S0-BYA-920

Minnie Muenscher's
Herb Cookbook

From Anise To Wormwood

There's garlic for pungency . . . and parsley to make the garlic bearable for your friends . . . rosemary for unforgettable scrambled eggs . . . and lavender tea for a unique midday lift. The calendulas in your back yard can float their petals in a festive punchbowl or stand in for costly saffron. And easily-grown chives will add spice to hors d'oeuvres, soups, salads or stews.

There is no limit to the use of herbs in preparing the full range of foods — and Minnie Muenscher's seven decades of experience with them makes her book an unequaled guide to the world of natural seasoning and fragrance.

Other Keats and Pivot Books of Relevant Interest

Guide to Medicinal Plants by Paul Schauenberg and Ferdinand Paris

How to Make Your Own Herbal Cosmetics by Liz Sanderson

Traveler's Joy by Juliette de Bairacli Levy

Herbs, Health and Astrology by Leon Petulengro

Choosing, Planting and Cultivating Herbs by Philippa Back

Growing Herbs as Aromatics by Roy Genders

Making Things with Herbs by Elizabeth Walker

Eat the Weeds by Ben Charles Harris

Ginseng by Ben Charles Harris

Minnie Muenscher's Herb Cookbook

by **Minnie Worthen Muenscher**

with illustrations by Elfriede Abbe

Keats Publishing, Inc.
New Canaan, Connecticut

MINNIE MUENSCHER'S HERB COOKBOOK

Copyright © 1978 by Cornell University
Illustrations copyright © 1955 by Elfriede Abbe

First published in 1978 by Cornell University Press
Pivot Health Edition published in 1980 by arrangement with
Cornell University Press

All Rights Reserved. No part of this book may be copied or reproduced in any
form whatsoever without the written permission of Keats Publishing, Inc.

ISBN: 0-87983-216-9
Library of Congress Catalog Card Number: 77-90908

Printed in the United States of America

KEATS LIVING WITH HERBS SERIES books are published by
Keats Publishing, Inc., 36 Grove Street, New Canaan, CT. 06840

To my daughters, Elizabeth, Helen, and Joanne
Also to my grandchildren
Ralph and Peter; Virginia and Fred; Seton, Chris, and Ann
AND TO ALL HAPPY COOKS

Contents

Acknowledgments

My thanks go forth daily to the many friends, known and unknown, who have added to my enjoyment of herbs. Many have given me recipes, and I have given credit where the recipes are used—thank you. Some recipes have come from almost next door, others from as far away as Lima, Peru; some are from friends I have never seen but who have shared their herbal information and recipes through a Round Robin of the Herb Society of America. I am also grateful to the nearby friends who have willingly sampled food as I tested recipes; I hope it has given them an increased appreciation of herbs; I'm pleased that they have seldom recommended that I change a recipe. Thanks, too, to the members of the Wednesday Night Supper Group at the Unitarian Church of Ithaca, New York, and to those of the Olympia Fellowship's Beacon Books Club who have approvingly sampled many a dish with an unfamiliar herb.

A few recipes, with an herb or two added, have come from cookbooks or pamphlets; permission to use them has been gratefully received. Especial thanks go to *Woman's Day*. In March 1958, they printed my "1200 Ways to Scramble an Egg"; "Herb Bread" in January 1961; "Cooking with Herb Seeds," May 1963; and "Breads That Are Different and Delicious," February 1969. Recipes from these articles, or adaptations of them, are reprinted here by permission of *Woman's Day Magazine,* a Fawcett publication. I am grateful for this permission and for the encouragement of Cora Anthony, at that time an associate editor.

The Review and Herald Publishing Association has kindly given me permission to use recipes from the series "Herbs throughout the Year," which appeared in *Life and Health,* January, March, May, August, September, and November 1964, and from the monthly series of 1966, "The Herb of the Month." I am glad to have this permission and appreciate the encouragement of Mary Castor Knight, then assistant editor of *Life and Health*.

The first recipe of mine to be printed was "Toast and Eggs" in the juvenile section of a Grange cookbook, published in 1908. With a few changes, I still use it occasionally for supper and have included it here.

The late Wilma Lord Perkins graciously gave me permission to adapt the recipe for "Devil's Food Cake II" from Aunt Fannie Farmer's *The Boston Cooking-School Cook Book.* In 1914 I studied that book in a college class. It has been constantly revised since then and has remained a popular cookbook.

Years ago I made a list and tables of suggested uses of herbs in the kitchen for the herb table at the Unitarian Church bazaar in Ithaca, New York. It first appeared in print as "Herbs for the Kitchen," *Museum Service,* Bulletin of the Rochester Museum of Arts and Sciences (now the Rochester Museum and Science Center), Vol. 32, pp. 138–139, October, 1959, Rochester, New York.

The Tillamook, Oregon, County Creamery Association gave permission to include their recipe for cheese cookies. Helen Ross Russell gladly gave me permission to use the "Rose Petal Honey Butter" recipe from her book *Beginner's Guide to Foraging for Dinner,* and Erika Gaertner was also happy that I wanted "Rose Hip Syrup" from her *Harvest without Planting.* Both authors studied economic botany at Cornell University under my husband.

Lois O'Connor, too, has kindly granted permission to reprint "Gazpacho La Quinta" from her book *Of Tarragon, Thyme, and Tauvirg.*

The following persons have given me no recipes and have eaten none of my herb-seasoned foods but have given me much appreciated help. I was concerned about the possible poisonous qualities of a few herbs and wrote about them to W. J. Dress of the Liberty Hyde Bailey Hortorium of Cornell University. He turned my letter over to Peter A. Hyypio, who does much of the extension work for the Hortorium. I appreciate his comments on rue, tansy, southernwood, and wormwood, plants that are mentioned in the sections "22 More Herbs to Cook With" and "Warnings about Using Herbs."

Helen Fossum, a retired professor from the University of Puget Sound at Tacoma, Washington, has carefully read the manuscript and given helpful suggestions concerning the writing, which I was very glad to receive.

In correspondence with Carol H. Woodward, this herb cookbook was first thought of and planned. Thank you, Carol. And grateful appreciation to James Twiggs, Daniel Snodderly, and Elsie Myers

Stainton of Cornell University Press, who have made this book possible. I never thought that a visit to a publishing office could be as enjoyable as the time I spent with them in firming plans for *Minnie Muenscher's Herb Cookbook.*

My family is widely scattered, but we all worked on this book: Joanne Droppers, of Alfred, New York, typed the entire manuscript; Elizabeth Muenscher, of Berkeley, California, and Helen Tryon, of Boulder City, Nevada, helped in the final reading of the manuscript. Thanks to my daughters, it is now completed.

I am delighted that the illustrations in this book are from woodcuts Elfriede Abbe made for my husband's book *Garden Spice and Wild Pot-Herbs.* Many of them are of herbs that grew in our garden in Ithaca. Thank you, Elfriede.

Last of all I want to express my daily gratitude to two who are no longer with me but whose influence permeates every page of this book. My mother, Trina Tobiassen Worthen, taught me that cooking is both a useful and a joyous occupation. My husband, Walter Conrad Muenscher, shared with me his love of herbs and of life.

M.W.M.

Olympia, Washington

Introduction

This is the book I wanted years ago when I started to cook with herbs. I believed then, as I do now, that herbs add fun as well as fragrance and flavor to cooking. But if I wanted to cook with an herb—basil for instance—it seemed I had to spend as much time hunting for a recipe to use as I did with the actual cooking. I soon adopted the following method for herb cooking: Smell the herb, taste it, decide with which foods it will be the most compatible, then make up a recipe using that herb. I recommend this method if you are adventuresome or experienced, but you may prefer the already tested recipes included here. They have come from my kitchen, and most of the herbs have been grown in my garden. Caraway and other seeds, however, I have bought at the grocery store. A variety of fine herbs are now available in many groceries, or can be bought from an increasingly large number of companies that sell flower and vegetable seeds and plants.

This book introduces you to some of my culinary friends. May you enjoy them as much as I do. I suppose that in a cookbook one should say: "Be sure to follow each recipe exactly as given, both to the amount of each ingredient and to the time of cooking." I cannot say this. I've told you how I do it, but you may like your coffee cake sweeter than mine, or may want more salt in your beef stew. You may like your casseroles a pale brown or richly colored; either way is right. When you have followed a recipe just as it is written, you may decide that for you, as for me, it is just right; or you may decide how to alter it the next time you use it. Best of all, it may suggest an entirely new recipe to you.

I expect that you will have fun cooking with herbs. That it may be fun instead of failure, I should warn you to be careful not to use too much of any herb. Until you know that you and your family like a certain herb, start with less than the recipe calls for, adding a little more each time until you find the amount that seems just right for you. It has been said that the best use of herbs is when they enhance the flavor without adding a distinctive taste of their own. While increasing the pleasure of cooking and the flavor of food, herbs add a delightful fragrance to the kitchen, often to the entire house. After I've baked herb bread, I may go out into the garden and be greeted by a welcoming fragrance when I come back in.

With many of these recipes I have suggested other herbs to use, other variations of the recipe. And with many recipes for a specific herb, I have suggested other uses for that herb. Part of the fun in cooking is creating variations of old standby recipes.

You will not cook long with herbs before you find out which ones you and your family like best. I trust that you will find here many recipes that you all like. And I hope, too, that you will experience the exhilaration which comes with creating new recipes, and that herbs will add flavor to your food, fragrance to your home, and joy to your life.

The body of this book comprises 40 herbs with recipes for each. To make the book more useful I have included numerous other comments and suggestions: (1) a short tribute to herbs; (2) directions for growing herbs indoors and outdoors and for drying and freezing herbs; (3) suggestions for using herbs in a salt-free diet; (4) general recipes and directions that apply to many herbs; (5) uses of ten basic herbs—displayed as end papers; (6) a metric conversion chart; and (7) an herbal bibliography.

In foods calling for shortening, either butter or margarine can be used. In many recipes I mention margarine only, where it will blend well with the other ingredients. Butter of course could be used if preferred.

Dried or frozen herbs can be used in place of fresh herbs. Sometimes specific directions are given in the recipe. A general rule is to use an equal amount of frozen in place of fresh herbs, but use one-third of the amount given in the recipe if you substitute dried herbs for fresh.

To make it easier for you to find what you can do with a given herb, I have arranged this book alphabetically by herbs rather than by foods. In this, my book differs from most other cookbooks. Since many herbs are mentioned as substitutes for other herbs, I have included these in cross references as well as in the index of herbs. When a recipe, herb bread for instance, calls for several herbs, the recipe is given in the section for the herb first named, but cross references to the recipe are given under the other herbs used. The cross references at the end of each herb section are, first, to other herbs or other recipes among the "Recipes for 40 Culinary Herbs"; second, to recipes in the section "Basic Recipes for Supplementary Foods."

You may want a recipe for herb waffles (I hope you do!) or you may wonder which herbs to use in molasses cookies. To help with this, you will find a food index. And since you may know an herb by its scientific rather than its common name, an index of scientific names is included also.

May herbs bring happiness to your home!

Herbs and the Friendly Garden

A Tribute

Herbs—gifts—the friendly garden.

Not all gifts from the herb garden are tangible. There is a kinship of soul among the growers of these fragrant plants. Some of the aroma of the herbs seeps into correspondence about the "hows" and "whats" of growing herbs. People you have never seen become dear friends.

Herbs—shared inspirations—the friendly garden.

More than any other part of the garden, the herbs speak of the past. Pick a leaf of costmary; rub it between your fingers. Our Pilgrim Mothers called it Bible Leaf and placed the long fragrant leaves in their Bibles. Its pungency kept them awake through seemingly endless sermons. See the chives with their dainty lavender flower heads. Clumps of chives are found, along with lilacs and peonies, in old forsaken farmyards. Why is southernwood dear to me? It grew in my grandmother's garden.

Herbs—memories—the friendly garden.

Herbs for present joy, for present beauty. Herbs for memories of long ago. And herbs for hopes of the future. I hope that some day a granddaughter will walk with me in this garden and I will say to her, "Smell that thyme! Years ago, your mother, on sunny summer days, took her afternoon nap under the apple tree on a thick fragrant bed of this thyme." And I hope that something of the peace, the fragrance, the joy of today and of yesterday will pass down the years, by way of the herb garden, to this child of the future.

Herbs—hope for tomorrow—the friendly garden.

Growing Herbs Outdoors and Indoors

Herbs are really undemanding plants. They can be grown among flowers, in the vegetable garden, or in special beds. They like a well-drained, friable soil. I have succeeded, however, in growing them in heavy clay and also in dirt that when dry looked like pure dust. Most herbs like a sunny location, and I have grown certain herbs where they received plenty of sunshine; but where that was not available I have grown the same herbs in semishade or even in rather heavy shade. Sweet woodruff likes the shade. Most herbs do not require as much watering as flowers and vegetables, but do not let them become absolutely dry for long. The mints like more moisture than most herbs.

Herbs are seldom bothered by insects or disease, especially if they are not crowded and air circulation is good. I fertilize mine lightly in the spring, sometimes again after I have harvested the leaves and hope for a second crop. They respond well to a little fertilizer, organic or chemical, but if they grow too luxuriantly they will have less fragrance and flavor, and fragrance and flavor is what we want from herbs. They do need to be weeded, but this is a pleasant task as one enjoys their perfume while working.

After a killing frost, I can still cook with fresh herbs, because I have already potted the annuals that I like as well as a few perennials. On the kitchen window sill or in a heated and lighted storage room I have basil, chives, marjoram, mint, oregano, sage, summer savory, and thyme. Rosemary, lemon verbena, and several different fragrant-leaved geraniums are with other house plants in the living room.

I will watch these plants closely for plant lice and other insects that they may have brought indoors, and spray them with rotonone if necessary. I'll water them every day or two, since the soil dries out quickly indoors, and sprinkle them frequently or hold them under the faucet, running slightly warm water over the tops, holding the pots at an angle so the soil will not wash out. I'll give them a little fertilizer each month, for they soon use up the nourishment in the soil.

If I did not have herb plants to bring indoors, I would plant seeds in the spring to have fresh herbs in the winter; if I forgot to do it in the spring, they could be started later. Most important of all, I will pinch off the tops frequently to keep them from becoming too tall and spindly.

Seeds for an herb window garden or for outdoor planting can be secured from a number of companies that sell garden and flower seeds. Local florists also may have seeds of annual herbs and potted plants of the perennials.

Further specific information on growing and preserving herbs is given under each herb in the "Recipes for 40 Culinary Herbs." For more detailed instructions consult the publications in the section "Books about Herbs."

Drying and Freezing Herbs

Herbs may be preserved by drying.

When the plants are just about to bloom is the best time to harvest leaves for drying. I pinch off the top two or three inches from each stem (I probably miss some); in a few weeks I can do this again; most summers I have at least three, possibly four, crops. I wash the sprigs in cold water to remove any dust or insects, pat them dry with a soft towel, and place them on a wire window screen on the arms of a chair in the shade, thus allowing air to reach them from all sides. I cover them with another screen. Cheesecloth could be used instead to cover them, or they could be spread on newspaper and covered with cheesecloth.

I could have cut the plants back to a few inches from the ground but not so low that all leaves were removed. If this is done at the beginning of blossoming, there will probably be a second crop. The cut branches can be dried the same way as I dry the leaves, or they can be tied in small bunches and hung in an attic or any shady place where there is good circulation of air. I have sometimes hung them during the daytime on the shady side of a tree. They should never be dried in sunshine because the sun will evaporate the oil and with the oil the flavor. I should not say "never" for it is sometimes well to finish the drying for half an hour or so in hot sunshine if the leaves are not completely dry. If there is any question about their dryness, and no sunshine, I finish them in the oven at the lowest possible temperature and with the door open. I have learned by experience that if not cracklingly dry they may mold, and that if the oven is too hot, they may turn an unappetizing brown.

When completely dry, they should be stored in covered containers. Baby-food jars are fine for this; large-mouthed pill bottles can be used. You may want to rub the leaves through a sieve before putting them into a jar, but the flavor is supposed to be the best if they are stored whole. I crumble mine as I use them. I have a small mortar and pestle but I usually put them into the palm of my left hand and crush them with my right thumb.

I label each jar before storing it; I also label the herbs before drying if I do more than one kind at a time. If the herbs are for gifts or to be sold at a bazaar, it is well to state on the label a use for the herb such as "Basil—Tomato." Some herbs lose their flavor in a year or two; it is a good idea to date them and to use them freely enough so that you need to replace them at the end of the year.

To substitute dried for fresh herbs in a recipe, use one-third of the amount given.

Freezing also preserves the flavor and the color of herbs. Parsley and mint, as well as other herbs, frozen in ice cubes add a festive touch to iced herb tea and other drinks. Any herb when frozen is good also in cooked foods. Use the same quantity as of fresh herbs. Pick the leaves when at their best, just before blossoms are opening. They do not need to be blanched. Wash the leaves, pat dry with a soft towel, and freeze them. They will separate easily if they are spread on a cooky tray, frozen, and then packed in wax paper or small plastic bags or containers. Thus you may remove only the amount you wish to use at one time. If you like a certain mixture of herbs for a certain recipe, mix these together before freezing.

I like to make a very strong mint or parsley tea; freeze this in an ice-cube tray; remove from the tray and store in a plastic bag. In the winter add a cube or two of the mint to boiling water and have a fine tea. The same can be done with parsley. It makes a refreshing tea. Or add parsley cubes to soup, casseroles, or hot tomato juice.

Fresh, frozen, or dried herbs may be used in most recipes. To substitute dried herbs for fresh, use one-third of the amount in the recipe. To substitute frozen herbs for fresh, use the full amount given in the recipe. To use frozen or fresh herbs instead of dried, substitute three times the quantity of dried herbs.

Herbs in the Salt-free Diet

For ten years I cooked without salt. We all enjoyed our food during that time. My husband said the food tasted so good that he did not want a salt substitute; the rest of us added what salt we wanted at the table. I had worried about the reactions of the successive students who worked for room and board at our house in order to help pay their college expenses. But they too were satisfied. I've often read that herbs are a satisfactory substitute for salt—not only for invalids but for healthy people who are urged to cut down on salt in order to stay well. Nowhere, however, have I read which herbs to use instead of salt. The answer is to do as I did and use the herbs that you and your family like.

I found that vegetables with herbs added were acceptable without salt; sometimes I used one herb alone, sometimes I combined several. The same was true for cheese dishes, chicken, fish, and meat. For most herbs I used 1 teaspoon if dried, 1 tablespoon if fresh, in 6 servings; for some ⅓ spoonful was enough. *See chart below.* Desserts were no problem; they were actually improved with the addition of mint or other herbs. The herbs suggested in the following chart are not to be added to the herbs in the recipes of this book; they are just a bringing together of help for salt-free diets.

I no longer cook without salt but I use less than is called for in cookbooks, including this one; and I am pleased that guests seldom reach for the salt shaker.

Using Herbs Instead of Salt
(for 6 servings)

Cereal	Vegetables	Cheese, chicken, fish, and meat	Desserts
See recipe for Oatmeal Porridge under Mint	Add ⅓ teaspoon dried OR 1 teaspoon fresh	Add 1 teaspoon dried OR 1 tablespoon fresh	Add 1 teaspoon dried OR 1 tablespoon fresh
	basil	basil	mint
	chives	chives	
	marjoram	marjoram	Add 1 teaspoon whole
	oregano	oregano	
	parsley	parsley	anise seed
	savory	savory	caraway seed
	thyme	thyme	poppy seed
			sesame seed
	Add 1 teaspoon	Add ⅓ teaspoon dried OR 1 teaspoon fresh	
	coriander seed, ground	dill	
	sesame seed	garlic	
		leeks	
		rosemary	
		sage	
		shallots	
		tarragon	
		Add 1 teaspoon	
		sesame seed	

Note: To use a combination of herbs, adjust the quantities accordingly.

RECIPES FOR
40 CULINARY HERBS

Anise

Anise *Pimpinella anisum*

Anise has been considered one of our most precious herbs. It was a tithing herb in biblical times. A tax on the seed increased the exchequer in early England. It was used for flavor and fragrance in food and also medicinally, especially to improve the flavor of medicine. Anise suspended over the bed, it was once claimed, would give the sleeper a youthful look and prevent disagreeable dreams. Anise seed steeped in hot milk has been recommended for sleeplessness—it might be worth a try. Anise is still treasured in Europe and in the United States as a fine flavoring herb.

Anise leaves are used in cream sauces and fruit salads or to add a distinctive flavor to vegetable soups and cooked greens. Anise seeds are a part of Christmas baking in many homes; the seeds are also good in cakes or cookies any time of the year—mixed in the dough or sprinkled on top before baking. They are good in breads, especially rye bread and coffeecakes. A few seeds added to apple sauce, baked apples, vegetables, soups, or stews, or with eggs, cheese, meat, or fish are welcome. They add character to substitute coffee drinks and make a delicious tea (see Herb Tea).

Here are a few of my favorite recipes with anise. They may suggest other ways for you to use it.

Oatmeal

1 cup regular oatmeal	½ teaspoon salt
2 cups boiling water	½ teaspoon anise seed

Slowly stir oatmeal into boiling water. Add salt and anise seed. Cook 1 minute, stirring frequently. Reduce heat and simmer 5 minutes or longer. Serve hot with cream and sugar or butter and brown sugar. Yields 2 cups.

Pancakes

1 egg white	1 teaspoon anise seed
1 egg yolk	½ cup milk
1 tablespoon cooking oil	1 cup Bisquick

Beat egg white until almost stiff. In another bowl mix egg yolk, oil, anise seed, and milk; stir until well blended. Add Bisquick and stir. Carefully fold in egg white. Drop a tablespoon for each cake on greased, heated frying pan. Cook a few minutes until bubbly all over; turn and cook on other side. Serve hot with butter and syrup or with apple sauce.

Herbed Beets

1 tablespoon margarine	1 tablespoon lemon juice or
3 cups diced cooked beets	more
1 teaspoon salt	1 tablespoon sugar
1 teaspoon anise seed	

Melt margarine over medium heat. Mix other ingredients together and add to margarine. Cook over low heat 5–10 minutes or until well blended. Serve hot or cold.

Variations: Other herbs can be used: seeds of caraway, dill, or fennel; fresh or dried chives, parsley, summer savory, or tarragon. Vinegar may be substituted for lemon juice.

Anise Coffeecake

1 cake active dry yeast	2 eggs
1 tablespoon sugar	¼ cup sugar
¼ cup warm water	2½ cups flour
¾ cup milk, scalded	½ teaspoon salt
3 tablespoons cooking oil	¼ teaspoon whole anise seed

Dissolve yeast and sugar in water and let stand 10 minutes. Scald and cool milk; then add oil, eggs, sugar, and yeast mixture. Beat well. Continue beating as flour, salt, and anise seed are added. Let rise in warm place 1 hour. Stir well, pour into greased pan (8½ x 8½ x 2 inches) and let rise 1 hour. Crumble topping (*below*) over cake and bake at 375 F. 25 minutes, or until nicely browned.

Topping

¾ cup sugar	⅛ teaspoon whole anise seed
1 tablespoon flour	3 tablespoons margarine

Mix all ingredients well and chill while coffeecake rises. Then crumble by hand over cake.

Variation: Cardamom may be substituted for the anise seed in both the coffeecake and the topping. Use powdered cardamom or crush the seeds in a mortar.

Molasses Drop Cookies

½ cup margarine	2 cups flour
½ cup brown sugar	½ teaspoon soda
1 egg	1 teaspoon baking powder
¼ cup molasses	½ teaspoon salt
½ cup buttermilk	1 cup seedless raisins
1 teaspoon anise seed	

Blend margarine and sugar. Add egg, molasses, buttermilk, and anise seed; stir until well mixed. Sift in flour, soda, baking powder, and salt; mix well; stir in raisins. Drop a spoonful at a time on ungreased cookie sheet. (Use a teaspoon or a tablespoon depending on how large a cookie you want.) Bake at 350 F. 10–12 minutes.

Variations: Dates, chopped cooked dried prunes, or finely chopped apples may be used in place of raisins or in addition. Nuts may be added. Instead of anise use cinnamon, allspice, nutmeg, ginger, cloves, cardamom, or combinations of these.

Apple Pie

Crust

- ½ teaspoon anise seed
- ⅔ cup vegetable shortening
- 2 cups flour (preferably unbleached)
- ½ teaspoon baking powder
- 1 teaspoon salt
- 5 tablespoons cold water

Filling

- ¾ cup sugar
- 2 tablespoons flour
- 1 quart peeled, sliced tart apples
- ½ teaspoon anise seed
- 1 tablespoon lemon juice (optional)

To make the crust, add anise to shortening; sift in dry ingredients, add water, and mix well. Form into a ball. Roll a little more than half the dough for the lower crust; fit into 9-inch pie pan with a little extending all around edge of pan. Roll top crust out and cut slits for steam to escape. For the filling, mix ½ cup of the sugar with the 2 tablespoons flour and sprinkle on lower crust. Add apples, sprinkle with anise, remaining ¼ cup sugar, and lemon juice. Moisten edge of lower crust; place top crust over all; trim if necessary and crimp edges together. Bake at 375 F. about 50 minutes, until crust is browned.

Variations: This pie is good without any herb or spice or with powdered dry mint or finely cut fresh mint, or with ground cardamom seed. Whole caraway or poppy seeds could be used; also a very little cumin or a teaspoon of fenugreek seed would be a delightful change.

See also Chocolate Cookies (Lemon Verbena), Cocoa Family Style (Cardamom), Coffee (Cardamom), Sugarless Cookies (Cardamom); *and* Herb Honey, Herb Tea.

Basil

Basil   *Ocimum basilicum*

The use of basil in cooking is rapidly increasing in the United States. It has been estimated that the increase was 3,000 per cent in recent years. We have no monopoly on its use; Italians, Portugese, and Spaniards use it in their native foods; in France it is called *herbe royale* (royal herb) and in Germany *Konigskraut* (King's plant). Its value in medicine and magic has been argued by physicians and scientists for thousands of years, but there is no cause to argue over its use as a seasoning for foods. It adds a pleasantly pungent flavor to soups, salads, casseroles, almost any protein food—cheese, fish, poultry, eggs, meats—and combines well with vegetables; some cooks say always with tomatoes, often with other vegetables. Like all herbs, try it first cautiously, adding more as you learn how good it is. Does it have a lemony-anise quality, a peppery clovelike taste, or just resemble anise?

I use basil almost anywhere in my cooking except in desserts. Some day I will make a chocolate basil ice cream and then I will know that it can also be used in desserts. I use it most often with vegetables and most of all with tomatoes. I should like to quote from an article of mine, "Basil," which appeared in *Life and Health* for July 1966: "Finely snipped fresh basil is a treat on garden-fresh tomatoes. Dried basil in tomato juice is equally refreshing. Stewed tomatoes with a tablespoon of thick cream, a slice or two of crumbled dry bread, and a sprinkling of basil is delicious. A casserole of zucchini squash, onions, tomatoes, and basil tastes as good as it smells while baking. I have not mentioned the amount of basil to use. It depends on how much you like. . . . A suggestion of basil is, as a friend would say, 'fantastic good.' Too much is 'a minor tragedy.' " Now for some other ways to use basil with tomatoes.

Tomato Juice

2 cups strained tomatoes, fresh, canned, or frozen

½ teaspoon dried basil OR 1½ teaspoons minced fresh basil

2 cups broth or bouillon

Salt and pepper to taste

How much salt and pepper to use depends upon how much is already in the tomatoes and soup or bouillon. Mix well. Chill before serving. It can be served hot: bring to a boil; pour into cups and top, if desired, with whipped cream or substitute, or float popcorn on top.

Tomato Salad Dressing

1 cup peeled, sliced tomatoes
2 teaspoons vinegar
3 tablespoons salad oil
½ teaspoon salt

½ teaspoon sugar
¼ teaspoon dried basil
½ teaspoon pepper

Combine all ingredients in blender and run on high until smooth—about ½ minute.

Bran Muffins

1 cup buttermilk
1 cup bran
1 egg
1 tablespoon molasses
3 tablespoons cooking oil

1 teaspoon basil
1 cup flour
2 teaspoons baking powder
½ teaspoon soda
1 teaspoon salt

Combine buttermilk with bran and let stand 5 minutes. Add egg, molasses, oil, and basil, and beat well. Sift in flour with baking powder, soda, and salt. Combine wet and dry ingredients and stir well. Fill greased muffin pans ¾ full. Bake 25 minutes at 375 F., or until nicely browned. Yields 8−12 muffins.

Split Pea Soup

1 pound dried split peas
2 quarts boiling water
1 teaspoon basil

1 teaspoon salt
1 tablespoon margarine
1 cup evaporated milk

Combine all ingredients except milk in a pot and simmer 2½ hours. Stir occasionally and add more water as needed. Strain through sieve or beat with egg beater until smooth. Add milk, reheat, and serve hot.

Variations: Oregano, thyme, or sage can be used instead of basil, or 2 tablespoons of finely cut parsley or chives can be added just before serving. Some people prefer not to strain their pea soup.

Squash Soup

Mix equal parts winter squash (cooked until smooth and rather dry) with milk (fresh, dried, or evaporated). Season with salt and basil and bring to a boil. This makes a thick, nourishing soup. Add more milk if you want a thinner soup.

Scrambled Eggs (Basic Recipe)

1 egg (use 2 if they are small)
1 tablespoon milk
¼ teaspoon salt

Pinch of basil
1 teaspoon margarine

Beat egg and milk with a fork until well mixed. Add salt and basil. Melt margarine in a small skillet, pour in the egg, cook on low or medium heat, stirring frequently. I like to cook mine slowly for 5 or more minutes.

Variations: This is a basic recipe but can have many substitutions. Cream of mushroom soup or any other soup can be used instead of milk and salt or the liquid omitted. Any culinary herb can be used with or instead of basil—savory, oregano, marjoram, parsley, chives, tarragon, thyme, dill, or cumin are very good with eggs. Two tablespoons of cottage cheese or a teaspoon of vinegar are favorites with some. A bit of ham, bologna, or another meat, or some grated cheese can be added. Bacon fat or chicken fat are tasty substitutes for margarine.

Noodles and Chicken

3 cups cooked noodles
1½ cups diced chicken
1 can cream of mushroom soup
¼ cup diced green pepper

¼ cup minced onion
1 teaspoon dried basil OR 1 tablespoon fresh basil leaves

Cook noodles according to directions on package. Mix all ingredients, bring to a boil, and simmer for 10 minutes, stirring frequently.

Variations: Pour into a casserole and bring to bubbling point in oven. The casserole can be covered with buttered crumbs and baked at 375 F. until browned. Macaroni or other pastas can be substituted for the noodles, other herbs for the basil.

Meat Loaf with Spinach Stuffing

1 pound ground beef	1 teaspoon salt
½ cup crumbled dry bread	1 teaspoon dried basil OR 1 ta-
1 egg	blespoon finely cut fresh
½ cup milk, fresh, or reconsti-	basil
tuted dry, or evaporated	

Mix thoroughly; pack half in casserole; cover with spinach stuffing; add rest of meat; bake at 350 F. for 1 hour.

Spinach Stuffing

Chopped spinach, 1 cup if frozen or 2½ cups if fresh	1 cup dried bread crumbs
1 tablespoon onion, chopped	1 teaspoon dried basil
2 tablespoons celery, chopped	½ teaspoon salt
1 tablespoon green pepper, chopped	1 tablespoon margarine

Chop all vegetables fine (I use a blender, followed by bread crumbs, which practically cleans the blender). Melt margarine in small skillet; add vegetables and cook a few minutes while stirring. Combine all and spread on first half of meat mixture; then add rest of meat and bake.

Variations: This stuffing could be used with other meats or to stuff a chicken or turkey. Or bake separately as a spinach casserole. The meat loaf is good without the stuffing but is very popular with it.

Zucchini Squash Casserole

1 package frozen zucchini squash OR 2 cups cubed fresh squash cooked 10 minutes and drained (use young squash; do not peel or remove seeds)

1 tablespoon margarine	½ teaspoon basil
1 tablespoon flour	½ teaspoon salt
1 cup milk	2 tablespoons grated cheese
1 egg, beaten	1 tablespoon minced onion

Arrange squash in casserole. Make a white sauce of the margarine, flour and milk. Pour sauce slowly over the beaten egg, stirring steadily. Add basil, salt, cheese, and onion; pour over the squash. Bake at 325 F. until egg mixture has set, about 25 minutes. The onion and cheese can be omitted, or they can be considerably increased.

Variations: A pepper, seeds removed and diced, or sliced celery can be cooked with the squash. Bread crumbs and margarine can be put on top of the squash after it has been mixed with the white sauce. Chives, thyme, marjoram, or rosemary can be substituted for the basil. Other vegetables can be used. Corn or spinach makes a good casserole.

Basil Tea

2 cups cold water
1½ teaspoons dried basil OR 1 tablespoon minced fresh basil

Bring water & basil slowly to a boil and steep 5 minutes. For an iced drink, cool, add 1 teaspoon lemon juice and 1 teaspoon (or more) sugar, pour into glasses, and add ice cubes. Try sweetening with honey instead of sugar.

See also Batter Bread (Parsley), Deviled Eggs (Chervil), Gazpacho La Quinta (Parsley), Lamb Stew (Leek), Macaroni for Salad (Comfrey), Pork Pie with Corn Bread Topping (Fenugreek), Potato Salad (Sorrel), Pot Roast with Thyme, Thyme in an Oven Roast; *and* Herb Butter, Candy, Herb Honey, Herb Jelly, Herb Vinegar.

Borage

Borage *Borago officinalis*

Borage, also called talewort and cool-tankard, is not as appreciated as it might be in today's kitchens. For many centuries it was one of the herbs most universally favored. Flowers of borage in wine was supposed centuries ago to bring gladness, increase memory, add a coolness to any drink, and "give a grace to the drynkynge"; moreover it was a symbol of courage.

The lovely blue flowers still add their beauty to cold drinks, and desserts, and salads; scattered over a dish of sliced tomatoes they are a joy to see; welcome, too, for their cucumberlike flavor. The leaves, also slightly cucumber flavored, are welcomed in salads and sandwiches by those who are allergic to cucumbers—also by those who have no allergies. Small plants and young leaves on older plants are fine for greens, resembling dark green spinach; the bristly hairs on the leaves disappear in cooking. Borage is claimed to be a substitute for parsley in seasoning soups and stews. The flowers can be candied by brushing both sides with beaten egg whites and dusting with granulated sugar.

I have not seen borage, either fresh or dried, in the stores but I plant plenty of it, with calendulas and nigella for color contrast, and use the flowers in my herb teas and in salads; the leaves in salads, sandwiches, soups, and stews. I dry some to use in winter. I hope you will try borage for beauty and for flavor.

Tomato Soup

2 tablespoons margarine	1 tablespoon finely cut borage leaves
2 tablespoons flour	½ teaspoon salt
3 cups hot milk	⅛ teaspoon pepper
1 can tomatoes (1 pound 13 ounces) OR 2 cups sliced ripe tomatoes	½ teaspoon sugar
1 tablespoon finely cut onion	2 tablespoons minced chervil OR parsley

Melt margarine and blend in flour. Remove from heat and slowly stir in milk. Return to heat and bring to a boil, stirring constantly until thickened. In the meantime simmer tomatoes, onions, borage, and seasonings (except the chervil or parsley) 10 minutes; strain. Slowly add the strained tomatoes to the white sauce, stirring all the time. Again bring just to the boiling point and serve. Sprinkle chervil or parsley on each bowl of soup.

A Summer Sandwich

1 3-ounce package cream cheese
1 tablespoon mayonnaise
1 tablespoon finely cut borage leaves

4 slices bread, white, rye, cracked wheat, raisin, or other

Remove cream cheese from refrigerator half an hour or longer before making the sandwich, or warm it in a bowl of hot water for a few minutes. Mix well with mayonnaise and borage leaves. Spread between slices of bread.

See also Candied Leaves, Flowers, and Seeds; Herb Honey.

Burnet *Poterium sanguisorba* Salad Burnet

Burnet is another herb which was used centuries ago to flavor wine. Its feathery foliage can improve the appearance and the flavor of iced drinks today. For years I have grown burnet as an ornamental. The leaves are one of the finest to add to flower arrangements—at least they are one of my favorites. I have liked them in salads and drinks and thought that was all they could be used for. But recently I have found references to burnet as greens and in soups. Use just the fresh young leaves before the plant blossoms. If the plant is kept from blossoming, it will form tender leaves for a long time; but if allowed to blossom, it will have most interesting seed heads. Only young leaves should be used for greens—preferably under 4 inches in length. Minced leaflets are good in butter for sandwiches or to add to vegetables, especially if a little thyme or some parsley is added.

Burnet has well been called a salad herb. Sprigs of leaves can line the salad bowl; fresh young leaves are a delicious cucumbery addition to potato salad, in fact to any vegetable or meat or fish salad. A teaspoon of minced burnet is fine in French salad dressing, and equally good in mayonnaise or other salad dressings. Burnet vinegar is good to use when making your own salad dressing—I have found it in grocery stores but I like to make my own (*see* Herb Vinegar). Burnet is one of the herbs used to flavor tea or to make herb tea (*see* Herb Tea).

See also Herb Butter, Greens, Garnishes.

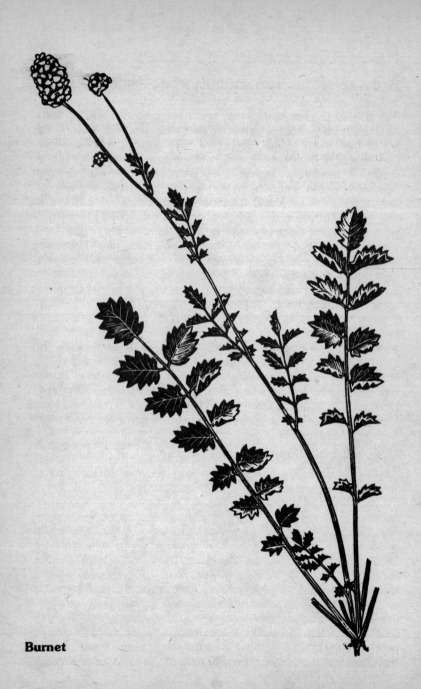

Burnet

Calendula   *Calendula officinalis*

Calendulas are sometimes known as Mary's Gold, more often as pot marigold. There are interesting explanations for its names. Calendula is from the Latin word "calends," meaning throughout the months because they bloom for many months, often flowering after frost has killed most annuals. *Officinalis* with the name of any plant means that plant is or has been used for medicine. In medieval times calendulas were thought to have great potency as a medicine, driving out poisons, strengthening eyesight, protecting from pestilence. Mary's Gold describes the brilliant yellow and orange colors of the petals. They were called pot marigolds because the leaves were a potherb, one that was cooked in a pot for greens. The calendula or pot marigold is not to be mixed up with Tagetes, the French and African marigolds—so far as I know these have no culinary values.

Are these names still valid? I think they are. Calendulas bloom in my yard from early summer almost to early winter; then they are moved indoors to bloom for a few more weeks. I do not know about their pharmaceutical properties, although I'm told they are used in cold creams and hair dyes; I do know that a glimpse of their sunny flowers is good medicine for the doldrums, that a few petals on top of a fruit salad can bring joy on a hot and muggy day. Mary's Gold—yes, plant breeders have extended the color range from deep orange to cream, but the typical yellow is still pure gold. Pot marigold—yes, we may not want to rob the plant of enough leaves for a "mess" of greens, but a few leaves added to other greens, comfrey or sorrel for instance, are good.

Calendulas can add color and taste to any recipe that calls for saffron—also to many other recipes. The claim is made that in pioneer days the grocer had barrels of dried petals because so many cooks wanted to add them to broths, soups, and stews. Now we must grow our own (an easy, pleasant task) or buy them from a florist. We can add them to desserts, especially custard, gelatin, and rice, or to cake or cookie batter. We can blend them into butter or cream cheese. We can cut the petals fine and use them as a garnish on any salad, or mix them into a sandwich spread. We can float fresh petals in punch or lemonade, make tea of the dried petals and the dried "buttons" from the center of the flower, or add them to other herb teas, especially mint tea. The flavor is stronger in the dried flowers, so start with a little. These are suggestions on how to bring calendula's sunshine into your kitchen.

Oyster Stew

1 pint oysters, with liquid
1 quart milk
¼ cup margarine
¼ teaspoon salt

2 tablespoons minced calendula petals OR 1 teaspoon dried calendula flowers

Simmer oysters in their liquid until the edges curl. Scald the milk. Combine the two and bring just to a boil. Add margarine, salt, and calendulas. Serve very hot. Pepper or paprika can be added.

Caraway

Caraway *Carum carvi*

Caraway is a biennial belonging to the carrot family. The first year it looks much like a carrot plant although its leaves are greener and smoother. Home-grown seeds, which will be harvested early the second summer, are stronger than the ones bought at a store. Also if one grows the plant, it is possible to use the tender leaves in salads and to boil the roots as a pleasant tasting vegetable. The roots resemble parsnips but are usually a little smaller. They are good boiled like parsnips or with parsnips. Their flavor is similar to that of the seeds but sweet and more delicate. The leaves and young stalks can be used for greens or combined with other greens. They are also used for salads or added to cooked vegetable salads.

Caraway is an attractive plant in the garden. The flowers are small, dainty, white or yellowish in umbels on stems that shoot up from the cluster of leaves. The plant as a whole has a delicate caraway fragrance.

It is best known and most widely used for its seeds, which are welcome additions to cakes, cookies, breads, puddings, desserts, and vegetables. They were used centuries ago for colic and to flavor bitter medicines. A toasted apple, spiked with caraway, was supposed to relieve indigestion. Rye bread with caraway seeds, also caraway in sauerkraut, in cheese, and in drinks, especially the kümmel of Germany and Russia, are standard ways of using the seed.

There was a time when caraway was thought to strengthen vision and to improve or preserve one's memory. Whether this is true or not, it is a valuable plant to have in the garden and a fine herb for the kitchen shelf. Here are a few of my favorite recipes using caraway. Perhaps they will suggest to you other ways in which you may use it.

Caraway is almost traditional in sauerkraut but it is good in cabbage, no matter how cooked, and in other vegetables—potatoes, tomatoes, turnips, onions, beets, and probably others. The next three recipes will suggest ways of using caraway to season vegetables; I hope they will suggest still other ways to you.

Red Cabbage

6 cups red cabbage, sliced (it cooks down amazingly)	2 tablespoons brown sugar
1 tart apple, diced (optional)	1 tablespoon caraway seed
1 cup boiling water	¼ cup or more of sliced Italian-style sausage (also optional)
1 teaspoon salt	1 tablespoon flour (optional)
2 tablespoons vinegar	

Bring cabbage and apple to a boil in the salted water. Pour into casserole with a cover (or use heavy foil for a cover); add vinegar, sugar, and caraway seed, plus sausage if you wish; stir well. Cover and bake 1 hour at 350 F.; the slow cooking blends the flavors. If too thin, sprinkle on flour, stir well, and bake uncovered for another 10 minutes.

Onion Pie

I like to read cookbooks and I often find recipes that suggest fine food to me. I found one I liked that dates back to the early 18th century. It is for onion pie. I use baking powder biscuit for the crust and made several other changes in it. You may want to change my recipe in various ways. It is not a dessert but a hearty vegetable dish.

Biscuit dough	1 egg
3 cups onions, peeled and thinly sliced	½ cup milk or cream
3 tablespoons margarine or other shortening	1 teaspoon caraway OR ½ teaspoon cumin
	Salt and pepper to taste

Line a pie plate with biscuit dough or, if you wish, with pie crust (fairly thick). Cook onions in the margarine at low heat until lightly browned. Cool slightly and spread over dough. Beat egg in milk; add caraway, salt, and pepper; pour over the onions. Bake at 400 F. until lightly browned, 15–20 minutes.

Variations: Grated cheese or crisp crumbled bacon can be added a few minutes before taking the pie from the oven. You might try 3 eggs beaten into 1 cup sour cream instead of 1 egg and ½ cup milk or cream.

Corn Souffle

¼ cup butter or margarine
¼ cup flour
1 cup milk
1 pound can cream-style corn
4 egg yolks, well beaten

½ teaspoon salt
½ cup grated or finely cut
   cheddar cheese
1 teaspoon caraway seed
4 egg whites, stiffly beaten

Melt butter, add flour, mix thoroughly. Add milk and corn; cook, stirring constantly, until it thickens. Remove from heat. Temper beaten egg yolks with some of hot mixture; then add egg yolks, salt, cheese, and caraway seed to the sauce; stir to blend. Fold in stiffly beaten egg whites. Bake in greased 2-quart casserole at 325 F. until set, about 45 minutes. Serves 4. We like this for lunch. With home-made bread and a hot drink, it makes a complete meal.

Caraway is especially pleasing in cakes and cookies made with molasses and fruit and for these combined in desserts. Here are two of my favorite desserts. They are fine dish-to-pass meals. Better take along a copy of the recipe, for you are sure to be asked for it.

Molasses Upside-down Pear Cake

¼ cup margarine (half a stick)
1 cup light-brown sugar
1 quart jar of pears, drained OR
   1 large can of pears, drained

¼ cup caraway seeds

Scatter thin slices of margarine on bottom of a baking dish approximately 12½ x 9 x 2¼. Sprinkle with sugar. Light oven, set it at 375 F., and put pan in oven so as to blend butter and sugar while cake batter is being mixed.

¾ cup cooking oil
¾ cup molasses
2 eggs
2 cups unbleached flour
2 teaspoons baking powder

1 teaspoon soda
½ teaspoon salt
1 teaspoon ginger
¾ cup buttermilk

Combine oil, molasses, and eggs; beat well. Sift dry ingredients and add alternately with the buttermilk. Remove pan from oven. Place pears on butter and sugar; sprinkle with caraway seed. Spoon on batter, completely covering pears. Bake at 375 F. about 35 minutes, depending on how brown you like it. Serve hot or cold. Whipped cream, ice cream, or a custard sauce can be served over this, but we like it best fresh from the oven, without any additions.

Molasses Apple Delight

3 cups peeled, diced apples
1 cup flour
½ cup sugar
1 teaspoon baking powder
½ teaspoon soda
1 egg, beaten
¼ cup light molasses
1 tablespoon caraway seeds
¼ cup buttermilk

Put apples in bottom of baking dish and bake at 400 F. while preparing batter. Sift dry ingredients together; add egg, molasses, caraway seed, and buttermilk; stir well. Cover apples with batter, stirring slightly.

Topping

¼ cup softened margarine
¼ cup light molasses
½ teaspoon cinnamon

Mix all together and spread over pudding. Bake at 400 F. until apples are soft and pudding is brown, 30–40 minutes. Serve hot or cold with rich cream and sugar or vanilla ice cream.

Caraway Crinkles

¾ cup margarine
½ cup sugar
½ cup dark brown sugar, firmly packed
2½ cups flour
1 teaspoon baking powder
½ teaspoon soda
¼ teaspoon salt
½ teaspoon nutmeg
1 egg
¼ cup molasses
1 tablespoon caraway seed
Wheaties or other flake cereal, crushed

Cream together margarine and sugars. Sift flour, baking powder, soda, salt, and nutmeg together. Stir egg, molasses, and caraway seed into margarine and sugar mixture. Add dry ingredients, ¼ at a time, and mix well. Chill. Form into balls the size of a walnut. Dip each ball in crushed flakes and place on ungreased cookie sheet. Bake at 375 F. until well browned, 10–12 minutes.

Swedish Limpa (Rye Bread)

5–5½ cups self-rising flour
2 packages dry yeast
2 cups water
½ cup firmly packed light-brown sugar
2 tablespoons oil
2 teaspoons grated orange rind
1½ teaspoons caraway seed
1½ teaspoons fennel seed
2 eggs
2 cups rye flour
Oil

Stir together 3 cups flour and yeast. Boil water, sugar, 2 tablespoons oil, orange rind, caraway and fennel seeds 3 minutes. Cool until warm. Add to flour-yeast mixture and beat until smooth—about 2 minutes on medium speed of electric mixer, or 300 strokes by hand. Blend in eggs. Add 1 cup self-rising flour and beat 1 minute on medium speed, or 150 times by hand. Stir in rye flour and more self-rising flour to make a moderately stiff dough. Turn onto lightly floured board and knead until smooth and satiny, about 8 to 10 minutes. Shape into ball and place in lightly greased bowl, turning to grease all sides. Cover and let rise in warm place—80 to 85 F.—until doubled in bulk, about 1½ hours. Punch down, divide in half, shape into 2 balls. Let rise 10 minutes. Shape loaves, place in greased pans 8½ x 4½ inches, brush with oil. Let rise until doubled, about 1 hour. Bake in oven preheated to 375 F. about 45 minutes; cover with foil to prevent excess browning. Remove from pans immediately and brush with oil. Makes 2 loaves.

This recipe was given to me by Sally Arthur, an Herb Society of America friend. She did not say what the heat should be—from the time she bakes it, 30—35 minutes, I suspect it was at 400 F. I bake it longer and more slowly.

Caraway Tea

When I first heard of caraway tea it sounded queer and I did not try it for some time. Now I make it often, for I very much like its aromatic taste. Add 1 teaspoon caraway to 1 cup water—more or less caraway to suit taste. Add caraway seeds to cold water and slowly bring to a boil. Strain and serve. A little sugar or honey and a little lemon juice may be used. Or a tea bag can be added and steeped a few minutes. I like it best with just caraway and water.

See also Apple Pie (Anise), Batter Bread (Parsley), Chocolate

Chip Cookies (Poppy Seed), Chocolate Cookies (Lemon Verbena), Cottage Cheese Plus (Cardamom), Herbed Beets (Anise), Macaroni for Salad (Comfrey), Whole Wheat Bread (Sesame); *and* Herb Vinegar.

Cardamom   *Elettaria cardamomum*

Cardamom is sometimes spelled cardamon or cardamum. It is a member of the Zingiberaceae family, as are ginger and turmeric. Like ginger, cardamom sweetens the breath and comforts the stomach. It has a pleasant spicy taste and can be used in cooking wherever ginger is used.

Be careful not to use too much. One-fourth teaspoon of dried powdered cardamom for four servings is enough, but if you find after trying this that you would like more, you may gradually increase to a teaspoonful. It is considered an aromatic stimulant; a little in the morning coffee is a good eyeopener. It adds an appetizing aroma and a slightly pungent taste to cookies, coffeecake, breads, sliced fruit and fruit salads, cottage cheese, desserts, and drinks.

A Blender Breakfast

There are mornings when I want a good, stick-to-me breakfast and I want it in a hurry so that I can get busy in the garden. Then I bless my blender. I put the following into it, run it about a minute until all is completely blended, and I have a quick, complete meal.

1 egg	1 graham cracker
1 cup milk	1 banana
1 tablespoon molasses	Pinch of powdered cardamom

Variations: Use sugar or honey instead of molasses. Vanilla or a sprinkling of nutmeg or ginger is good in place of cardamom. If you use no seasoning, add a pinch of salt. Other fruit could be used instead of banana. Sometimes I leave out the graham cracker and eat a slice of toast or a couple of rye crisps while I drink this breakfast.

Cardamon with Vegetables

Its fragrant spiciness makes cardamom especially good in vegetables. Try a pinch or two in pea soup, mashed winter squash, sweet potatoes, cabbage or rutabagas—or any other vegetable.

Cottage Cheese Plus

Other names for this recipe might well be "My Mystery Dish," "A

Salad Meal," or "Dieters' Delight." It is a mystery, for I'll wager that nobody will guess what is in it; it is a salad that has protein, carbohydrates, fruit, and vegetables enough for a complete meal; it has a good share of vitamins and minerals but is short on fats and sugars. It can be changed in an endless number of ways, appealing to the cook's imagination and ingenuity.

1 large stalk celery	2 tablespoons seedless raisins
1 small onion, diced	1 tablespoon sesame seed
1 small apple (OR ½ a big one), diced	¼ cup granola
2 tablespoons nuts, chopped	2 tablespoons wheat germ
¾ cup cottage cheese	2 tablespoons orange Tang
	½ teaspoon powdered cardamom

Cut stalk of celery in two, lengthwise, then crosswise in thin slices, dice onion and apple, and chop nuts (I use walnuts, any kind would do). Place these and the cottage cheese in a big mixing bowl; add raisins, sesame seed, granola, wheat germ, and Tang; sprinkle with a few shakes of powdered cardamom (my cardamom comes in a can with a shaker top) OR add ½ teaspoon cardamom; stir until well blended. Serve as is or chilled.

Variations: Hard-cooked eggs or fish may be substituted for cottage cheese, but I prefer cottage cheese. Tomato, cucumber, or other vegetables could be added to, or substituted for, celery and onion. Almost any fresh or canned fruit (drain canned fruit) could be used with or in place of apple and raisins (banana for apple, dates for raisins). Any crisp cereal, or crumbled graham crackers or rye crisp, could be a substitute for granola. Almost any culinary herb or spice can replace, or add to, the sesame seed and cardamom—try caraway seed or poppy seed or powdered coriander. Wheat germ is optional; maybe you would prefer brewer's yeast for the added vitamins. An orange or ½ cup of canned mandarin oranges would be as good as the Tang. Perhaps you can think of other changes—it is, indeed, a versatile recipe.

Peach Cornstarch Pudding

3 tablespoons cornstarch	2 cups sliced peaches, fresh, frozen, or canned
1½ cups milk	¼ teaspoon powdered cardamom
2 egg yolks	2 egg whites, beaten stiff
½ cup sugar	
½ teaspoon salt	

Mix cornstarch with a little milk; scald remaining milk; gradually add cornstarch to hot milk, cook stirring constantly until thickened; remove from heat. Combine egg yolks, sugar, and salt, and stir slowly into the cornstarch-milk mixture; add peaches if fresh or frozen; return to low heat and cook 10 minutes, stirring very frequently (or cook longer in a double boiler, stirring frequently), until thickened and fruit is cooked. Remove from the heat; add cardamom and well-drained peaches if canned. Fold in well-beaten egg whites and just bring to a boil. Serve warm or chilled.

Variations: Chopped nuts or grated coconut can be sprinkled over each serving. Add 1 tablespoon lemon juice after egg whites; or use ginger instead of cardamom.

Cardamom can add flavor and interest to foods for any meal. One of my favorite ways to use it is in gelatin desserts. Here are two that I especially like.

Fruit Gelatin

1 cup fruit cocktail, well drained	2 egg yolks, beaten
1 envelope unflavored gelatin	1 cup light cream
½ cup sugar	2 egg whites
1 cup fruit syrup (add water if necessary)	¼ teaspoon ground cardamom (approximately)
2 tablespoons mint vinegar (OR lemon juice)	

Mix gelatin and sugar until well blended. Add syrup, vinegar, and egg yolks. Cook stirring constantly over low heat until thickened and gelatin is dissolved. Pour into large bowl to cool. Gradually add cream, stirring all the time. Chill until it begins to thicken. Beat until light and fluffy. Add fruit and fold in well-beaten egg whites. Sprinkle with cardamom and stir; sprinkle again and stir. Taste to see if you want a third sprinkling. (I hope your cardamom can has a sprinkler top.) This dessert can be made the day before serving and kept in the refrigerator.

Pineapple Cottage Cheese Dessert

1 envelope unflavored gelatin	¼ cup lemon juice
½ cup pineapple juice	1 cup drained crushed pineapple
¼ cup sugar	1 cup cottage cheese
Pinch of salt	½ teaspoon cardamom OR coriander
1 cup boiling water	

Soften gelatin in pineapple juice and heat to dissolve gelatin. Add sugar, salt, and boiling water; stir until entirely dissolved. Add lemon juice, pineapple, cottage cheese, and cardamom (or coriander); stir well. Mold and chill. Stir a time or two as it is thickening.

Variations: Nut meats, dates, and/or coconut can be added with the cottage cheese.

Cherry Molasses Cake

½ cup margarine (or butter)	1 cup buttermilk (fresh or reconstituted)
½ cup sugar	
2 eggs	1 21-ounce can instant cherry pudding or pie mix
½ cup molasses	
2 cups flour	½ teaspoon cardamom
1 teaspoon salt	1 cup graham cracker crumbs, well crushed
1 teaspoon soda	
1 teaspoon baking powder	¼ cup coconut
½ teaspoon cardamom	¼ cup nut meats

Mix margarine and sugar until well blended (easier if margarine has been at room temperature for an hour); add eggs and molasses and stir well. Sift flour, salt, soda, baking powder, and ½ teaspoon cardamom together; add alternately with buttermilk to margarine-sugar mixture. (Dried powdered buttermilk can be reconstituted by adding ½ cup plus 2 tablespoons to 1 cup water.) Spread in a greased pan, 9 x 12½ inches. Mix cherry filling and other ½ teaspoon cardamom; spread over the dough (drop a spoonful at a time and then spread carefully). Top with graham cracker crumbs which have been well mixed with coconut and nut meats. Bake at 350 F. approximately 35 minutes.

Variations: Add ½ teaspoon ginger to flour in the sifter, or use ginger or coriander in place of cardamom. Omit coconut and add more nuts. Canned or fresh pie cherries thickened with flour or cornstarch, sweetened to taste and seasoned as above, could be used instead of the canned cherry mix.

Sugarless Cookies

¼ cup strained honey	¼ teaspoon salt
¼ cup margarine or butter	½ teaspoon ground cardamom
1 egg	2 tablespoons chopped nut meats
½ cup plus 2 tablespoons flour	
3 tablespoons nonfat dry milk	2 tablespoons chopped dates
1 teaspoon baking powder	2 tablespoons coconut

Keep honey and margarine at room temperature for an hour or more or stand in a dish of hot water until soft. Mix very thoroughly (you may be surprised at how easily they blend); beat egg a bit in the bowl, then mix with the honey and margarine; sift in the flour, milk, baking powder, salt, and cardamom; mix well and then add the following, stirring after each addition: nuts, dates, and coconut. Drop by scant teaspoonfuls on greased cookie sheet. Bake 10 minutes, or until lightly browned, at 325 F.

Variations: Ground anise seed can be used instead of cardamom; or 1 tablespoon whole poppy or sesame seeds; good, too, with crushed mint, lemon verbena, or fragrant-leaved geranium leaves.

Cocoa Family Style

¼ cup cocoa
¼ cup sugar
½ teaspoon ground cardamom

1 cup boiling water
1 quart scalded milk

Thoroughly mix cocoa, sugar, and cardamom. Slowly add boiling water, stirring until all is dissolved. Bring to a boil and simmer 5 minutes. Add milk and bring almost to boiling point. (Reconstituted powdered or evaporated milk can be used instead of fresh milk.)

Variation: Good with anise in place of cardamom.

Rich Cocoa

Decrease the proportion of milk to sugar and cocoa. Add whipped cream or marshmallows to each serving. If chilled, either this cocoa or the Cocoa Family Style makes a good chocolate drink.

Coffee

Add a pinch of powdered cardamom or 2 or 3 crushed seeds to each cup of coffee before serving. This is especially appreciated in decaffeinated coffee or coffee substitutes. Try anise, or a very little coriander or cumin in coffee. If you like it, you may want to add a little more the next time.

See also Anise Coffeecake, Apple Pie (Anise), Carrot Cream Pie (Coriander), Green Tomato Mince Pie (Coriander), Molasses Drop Cookies (Anise), Orange Marmalade Bread (Coriander); *and* Herb Honey.

Chervil *Anthriscus cerefolium*

Chervil is an old-time herb that is becoming increasingly popular as a garnish similar to parsley and as a delightfully refreshing seasoning. With its delicate fernlike leaves, a bright green, it is a delight to see as well as to taste. Gardeners appreciate that it likes semishade and will grow even in shaded spots. Chervil may be a new herb to many but it is supposed to have been brought to the Mediterranean region from farther north about 300 B.C. and apparently has been appreciated and used in Europe ever since. Pliny, the great naturalist (A.D. 23–79), wrote that chervil is a remedy for hiccups. Time was when chervil supposedly added zest to living, made one less forgetful, wittier, happier. In the language of flowers it symbolizes sincerity. The name *cerefolium* means pleasant leaf.

Chervil was used by the ancient Greeks and Romans to season their food. It still is used as a wholesome herb to add zest to a great variety of foods, including soups, salads, fish, poultry, meat, fruit, and vegetables. Minced fresh leaves or crumbled dried leaves are added to foods before or during cooking. Some wise cooks add just enough to enhance the flavor of the food without adding a new taste. Chervil is especially adept at this; it also blends well with other herbs. Other cooks use enough to add the fine flavor of the herb. Many say this flavor is similar to parsley, others to anise, still others to tarragon, some to parsley plus licorice, some to parsley plus tarragon. I agree with those who say it has a delicious taste of its own, rich and slightly peppery.

Many who do not add chervil to their cooking welcome it as a garnish—sprigs of whole leaves for salads, fish, and meat; snipped leaves on soups, salads, and bowls of fresh fruit. Many regret that fresh chervil is not found more often in grocery stores; they would like to find it with the parsley and chives. Others regret that spice counters do not contain dried chervil. As a result many are growing chervil in their vegetable or herb gardens or in the flower beds or in pots on the kitchen window sill, glad that it does not demand sunshine and that they have the fresh leaves handy. If the outer leaves are cut, new leaves will grow. No matter how you use chervil, whether you can taste it or not, it should add interest to your cooking. Perhaps the ancients were right when they said it added zest to life—this added interest to foods may add zest to daily living.

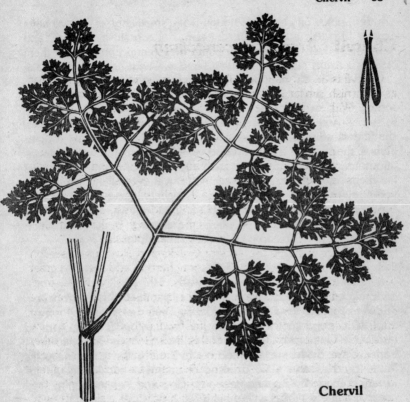

Chervil

You may find in your cookbooks reference to cooking chervil roots. This is a different plant, turnip-rooted chervil (*Chaerophyllum bulbosum*). It can be cooked like carrots or other root vegetables. I have not used it or even seen it and so have no recipes for it. I hope you will like the following recipes and that you will try using chervil sometimes as substitute for parsley or tarragon.

Chervil Biscuits

Chervil is good in biscuits, waffles, and other nonyeast breads. (*See* Marjoram Biscuits *and* Thyme for Waffles.) But it is also good alone or with other herbs in raised breads. Someday when you are baking bread, don't put all the dough into bread pans; save some for biscuits. Spread a pan generously with chervil butter (*see* Herb

Butter); pinch off chunks of dough (I like small chunks so I will have crusty biscuits); put them in the pan, not too close together, and turn them over (this gives you butter on top and bottom). Let them rise in a warm place until doubled in size, about half an hour. Bake at 425 F. 15–25 minutes, depending on size of biscuits.

Chervil Soup

Chervil soup can be made with vegetable or chicken stock or white sauce. Melt 2 tablespoons margarine; stir in 2 tablespoons flour and cook over low heat until well blended; slowly add 2 cups stock or milk, stirring all the time; add 3 tablespoons minced chervil; cook over low heat until it thickens, stirring almost all the time. If you have no chicken or vegetable stock in the refrigerator (saved from cooking), dissolve powdered bouillon or bouillon cubes in water, following directions on package for amount to use.

Deviled Eggs

Bring enough water to a boil to cover the eggs without crowding. Lower eggs into the water (a slotted spoon is fine, a tablespoon will do). Cover and cook eggs just below boiling for 15 minutes (rapid boiling 10 minutes). Drain; put in cold water immediately to cool. Shell eggs, cut lengthwise, and remove the yolks. Combine yolks with 1 tablespoon salad dressing or cream or pickle vinegar for every 2 eggs; add salt and pepper to taste and ¼ teaspoon minced chervil. Fill egg whites with mixture.

Variations: Paprika can be sprinkled on top. A little powdered or prepared mustard or horseradish can be added to the yolks. Other herbs, used alone or combined, can be added or substituted; basil, chives, marjoram, oregano, and parsley are recommended.

See also Egg Sandwich Filling (Shallots), Fish with Sorrel, Lavender Gelatin, Potato and Leek Soup, Potato Salad (Sorrel), Sorrel Soup, Tomato Soup (Borage); *and* Herb Butter, Greens, Herb Jelly, Herb Vinegar.

Chive *Allium schoenoprasum*

Chives, it is claimed, are one of the three most popular herbs in America. The others are parsley and spearmint. They were introduced into China (I do not know from where) 2,000 years ago. Two hundred years ago or more they were introduced into New England. Some of our forefathers planted them in their pastures so the cows would give chive-flavored milk. Such milk would not be popular today, but we do use the finely cut leaves as seasoning; the whole leaves as a garnish for vegetables, meat, fish, poultry, eggs, and cheese. Chives give a mild onion flavor to salads, soups, and stews; they are delicious sprinkled on an open-faced bread and butter sandwich, and beautiful in cottage cheese and baked potatoes.

They are one of the earliest plants to appear in the spring and can be used for many months directly from the garden. Instead of clipping the tops from the plants, cut off a few entire leaves. Chives can be grown indoors the year around if used frequently; cutting encourages tender new growth. They will do best in a cool, light place. Plants for the kitchen can be raised from seed, grown from clumps bought at the grocery, or brought in from the garden. You will have stronger plants if those from the garden are allowed to freeze before bringing the pots indoors. If you do not have freezing weather, I suspect that a few weeks in the refrigerator might be good for them. Chives can be dried or frozen for year-round use.

I have long used the leaves as an edible garnish and as a satisfying seasoner. Today I read that they can be used as a potherb. They do not seem to me to be substantial enough for greens, but they can be added to comfrey or chard for greens—about 1 part chives to 6 or more parts of other greens. I have also read that pickled chive bulbs are delicious; I believe this would be true, but the bulbs are so small that I would prefer to make pickles from onions.

All parts of the plant have the same mild onion flavor, so I agreed when I read that the flowers would be fine in omelets and scrambled eggs. This is not to suggest tossing the entire flower head into the eggs, but to separate the individual flowers from the cluster. I did not want to wait until I cooked eggs to try the flowers as a seasoner so I immediately tasted them, was delighted with the taste, and made myself a dainty and likable sandwich by picking off the

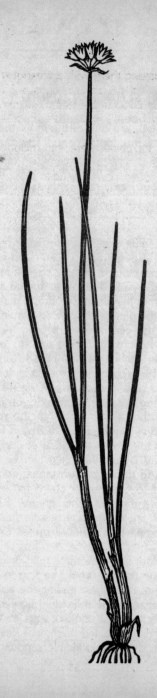

Chive

individual flowers, mixing them with a teaspoon of softened margarine, and spreading this on crackers. I have for years enjoyed the
purplish flowers as an ornamental feature in our gardens—always in
the herb garden, frequently with the vegetables, sometimes in a
flower border.

I give no recipes for chives here, but include cross references to
recipes using them and a list in the index of recipes where they are
used. I like to use chive often because it is a health-giving herb,
adds flavor to many foods, gives a welcoming odor to the kitchen,
and with its green leaves and colorful flowers enhances the beauty
of many foods.

See also Deviled Eggs (Chervil), Egg Sandwich Filling (Shallots),
Herbed Beets (Anise), Macaroni for Salad, (Comfrey), Potato and
Leek Soup, Potato Salad (Sorrel), Pot Roast with Thyme, Scram-
bled Eggs (Basil), Sour Cream Sauce (Horseradish), Split Pea
Soup (Basil), Stewed Chicken (Coriander), Thyme in an Oven
Roast, Zucchini Squash Casserole (Basil).

Comfrey   *Symphytum officinale*

Until a few years ago I had not heard of comfrey. Now it is one of
the important and frequently used herbs in my garden; in fact I
have it among the vegetables as well. I am surprised I did not know
about it, for it is reported to have been used by herbalists for at
least 2,000 years. At first it was only used medicinally, both inter-
nally and externally. Because of its capacity (due to a goodly
amount of allantoin) to speed the cure of fractures, it was called
"knit-bone." It is still considered one of the most important herbs
so far as health is concerned. It is particularly high in protein, rank-
ing above the important soy bean. Comfrey greens is a good dish
to have when beefsteak is too costly. It has a considerable amount
of minerals and vitamins: it is high in calcium, potassium, and phos-
phorus, with some iron, manganese, and cobalt; and is a good
source of vitamins A, B_{12}, and C. No wonder it is called the magic
herb and the healing herb.

By some it is grown as an ornamental in the flower garden. Not
long ago I saw a blossoming stalk of comfrey win a blue ribbon at a
garden club flower show. I like its blossoms, which remind me of its
close relative, borage. It is a sturdy member of the borage family
and grows rapidly. Because of its rank growth I give it plenty of
room toward the background. Some farmers have found it useful as
a mulch or compost plant; it is reported to increase both the quantity and the quality of the crops. It is equally useful for composting
flower beds. I bury leaves that I have used for tea in my garden,
putting them underground near my favorite herbs. Other farmers
grow comfrey to use as fodder for their animals. Since the feeding
of comfrey seemed to increase the health and strength of animals, it
was decided that "what is good for the piggies should be good for
the kiddies."

The most obvious uses seemed for greens and herb tea; for several years this was the only way I used comfrey, but I am exploring
more ways. I find a comfrey iced drink a delightful way to take my
vitamins and minerals.

Comfrey Soup

1 cup finely cut comfrey
2 cups boiling water
½ cup diced potatoes
1 teaspoon instant beef bouillon

1 tablespoon finely diced shallots, leeks, or onions
1 teaspoon margarine or bacon fat

Put all into kettle and cook approximately 10 minutes or until potatoes are tender. Strain if you wish.

Comfrey Greens

When I use comfrey, I usually add a few French sorrel leaves or its close relative, sour grass. I have a small place in the herb garden for sour grass (*Rumex acetosella*), but it takes occasional weeding to keep it in a small place. Some people like to add a few horseradish leaves or dandelion leaves to comfrey greens. *See* Greens.

Macaroni for Salad

1 cup finely cut comfrey
1 cup macaroni, small size
1½ cups boiling water

½ teaspoon salt
1 tablespoon margarine

Combine all ingredients and cook about 10 minutes or until macaroni is tender. The same proportions should be satisfactory with any macaroni, spaghetti, noodles, or rice.

Variations: This is the basis for salads made with chicken, fish, meat, or vegetables. Substitute other herbs for comfrey: use 2 tablespoons parsley or chives; not more than 1 tablespoon fresh basil, marjoram, or oregano; 1 teaspoon thyme or caraway seed.

A Summertime Drink

1 cup comfrey
½ cup mint
¼ cup French sorrel

3 cups cold water
3 tablespoons strained honey
1 tablespoon lemon juice

Cut fresh leaves into pieces about an inch long (a good drink may also be made by leaving the leaves whole). Combine comfrey, mint, sorrel, and water in a kettle; bring slowly to a boil; steep 5 minutes; strain. Add honey and lemon juice, chill, and serve with ice cubes. The response of guests has been enthusiastic.

Variations: If you do not have French sorrel, the sorrel weeds in your yard or garden can be used. If sorrel isn't available, use more lemon juice. Thyme—especially lemon thyme—is also suggested, and any of the mints add flavor to a summertime drink made with comfrey.

Comfrey Tea

With comfrey tea I add any of the mints. Of the 6 mints in my herb garden, for tea I usually choose peppermint, spearmint, apple mint, or lemon mint (also called orange mint or bergamot mint). *See* Herb Tea.

See also Calendula; *and* Horseradish Leaves, Sorrel Greens.

Coriander *Coriandrum sativum*

Coriander, Chinese parsley, is an important member of the parsley or Umbelliferae family. It was used in China as a culinary herb 1,500 years before Christ. Centuries later, in 1440, it was described in an early English gardening book by Mayster John Gardener. It is still a popular herb in many countries, especially China, India, Africa, and Peru. It is the Mexican's well-loved *cilantro*.

With its lacy leaves and delicate white, pink, and lavender flowers, coriander is a dainty addition to the flower bed. Its foliage does have a distinct buglike odor, although its seeds have a sharp, tangy fragrance and flavor which is increasingly strong the older the seeds become. Their lasting fragrance make the seeds a fine addition to sachets or fragrance bags; they are also used as breath sweeteners. Their spicy taste makes some medicines more acceptable. They added bite to the candy balls that delighted children fifty years ago.

Cooks in the United States usually use the seeds when they season with coriander. In Peru, probably in other countries, the young fresh leaves, finely cut, are added to soups and stews, cottage cheese, and other dishes. If you raise coriander in your herb garden, I suggest trying the leaves as a garnish and seasoning. I get the seeds at the grocery store, and use them in my coffee substitute, in bread, cake, cookies, pies, and puddings, occasionally with chicken, in meat sauce, and to season a number of vegetables.

Here are a few of my favorite recipes. I have read that the use of coriander "may be an acquired taste, but once it is acquired it may come close to being an addiction." I wish that all addictions were as pleasant and as beneficial.

Orange Marmalade Bread

This is a delicious rich bread. It can be served for dainty tea sandwiches but is equally good sliced thick and made into a hearty ham or peanut butter sandwich. Baked in small tins, wrapped in foil, it makes an excellent gift for a shut-in or as a hostess gift. Toast for breakfast. Serve with fruit salad.

2 packages yeast
2 tablespoons sugar
2 cups warm water
3 eggs
½ cup cooking oil
1 cup dried skim milk

½ cup wheat germ (optional)
1 teaspoon salt
2 tablespoons ground coriander seed
1 pound jar orange marmalade
8 cups flour (approximately)

Dissolve yeast and sugar in warm water; let stand 15 minutes. Add other ingredients but only 3 cups of the flour. Beat vigorously at least 2 minutes until smooth and well blended. Stir in most of the remaining flour as needed. Turn out on floured board and knead until smooth and satiny, about 10 minutes. Let rise in warm place until doubled in size, about 1 hour. Punch down, turn over in pan, and let rise another hour. Turn out on greased board; let rest 10 minutes; form into loaves and place in greased bread pans. Let rise until doubled in bulk, about 1 hour. Bake at 350 F. about 50 minutes, until brown and loaves leave pan easily.

Variations: Cranberries can be used instead of the orange marmalade (3 cups sliced berries, 1 cup of orange juice, and 1 cup sugar); mixture may need more flour. A tablespoon of cinnamon or of ground cardamom can be used instead of the coriander seed.

Spinach Soup

2 tablespoons margarine
2 tablespoons flour
1 package frozen chopped spinach
2 teaspoons instant chicken bouillon OR 2 chicken bouillon cubes
2 cups hot water

½ cup evaporated milk, undiluted
½ teaspoon salt
¼ teaspoon ground coriander
⅛ teaspoon pepper
½ teaspoon onion powder OR 1 tablespoon finely diced onion
Whipped cream (optional)

Melt margarine in large skillet or heavy-bottomed kettle. Stir in the flour over low heat so it does not turn brown. Dissolve bouillon in water and gradually stir into margarine and flour; cook, stirring constantly until thickened. Break up frozen spinach and add to sauce; cook 2 minutes after it comes to a boil. Add milk and seasonings and bring to a boil again. A tablespoon of whipped cream makes an attractive topping to each dish of soup, or use a whipped-cream substitute or sour cream.

Variations: For color contrast sprinkle the cream with finely cut parsley or chives (or add herbs without cream). For texture contrast

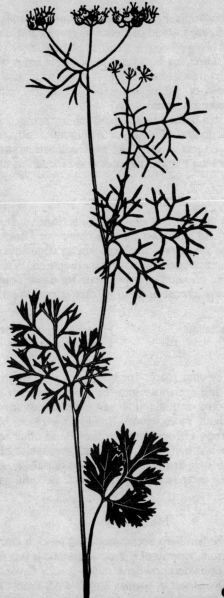

Coriander

top with chopped peanuts. For flavor contrast use crumbled cooked bacon or grated cheese instead of cream or on top of it. Try a bit of any of the other culinary herbs instead of coriander, or use a little nutmeg or mace. Omit the flour and thicken the soup by beating 2 egg yolks into the milk before adding it to the soup; use cream or half-and-half instead of evaporated milk, or add the spinach to a regular thin or medium cream sauce.

Further variety can be had by straining the hot spinach through a sieve or putting it in the blender for a minute. Fresh or canned spinach can be used just as well. Cut fresh spinach in small pieces before or after cooking it a few minutes and proceed as above.

Stewed Chicken

For many years this was one of our favorite Sunday dinners. The chicken either stewed while we were at church or I cooked it the day before. Frozen peas (or a fresh or canned vegetable from our garden) and mashed potatoes were quickly prepared. With a tossed salad or a vegetable tray and with ice cream for dessert our Sunday dinner at home was almost as easy as dining out. We thought it even more delicious.

1 stewing chicken (about 4 pounds)	1 teaspoon ground coriander
1 teaspoon salt	1 quart boiling water

Cut chicken into serving pieces (or buy it cut up). Wash and put chicken with salt and coriander into the boiling water. Cover and simmer about 2 hours or until tender (an older chicken needs more cooking but may have more flavor). Remove the pieces of chicken and thicken the broth. Onions, carrots, celery, and other vegetables can be added the last half hour; cook until vegetables are tender but not mushy. Sprinkle finely cut fresh leaves of parsley, chives, or coriander on top of each serving for a colorful, flavorful garnish.

Meat Sauce

Hamburger sauce is a very accommodating food. It can be used on noodles, macaroni, or any of the other pastas. It is a fine addition to cornbread or baking powder biscuits. It adds flavor to rice or baked potatoes. Over toast or waffles it makes an almost complete breakfast or lunch. It can be served after half an hour's cooking or it is even richer if simmered for 2 or 3 hours; but don't let it burn if you cook it a long time—look once in a while to see if a little water should be added. A cup (more or less) of leftover peas, beans, or corn can be added the last 15 or 20 minutes. Here is my recipe—change it as you please. I sometimes double it and freeze some.

1 tablespoon cooking oil	1 8-ounce can tomato sauce
½ cup sliced onions	1 teaspoon dried basil OR 1 tablespoon minced fresh basil
1 pound ground beef	
2 cups stewed tomatoes (1 16-ounce can) OR equal amount of diced fresh tomatoes	½ teaspoon ground coriander seed

Heat oil in a large skillet; add onion and stir, cooking until onions begin to turn yellow. Add beef and cook over medium heat, stirring constantly, until meat is no longer pink. Add remaining ingredients; stir well; bring to a boil; then simmer 2 hours or longer. If you want to cook it quickly, do not turn down the heat but do stir often. For slow cooking stir once in a while.

This is one of the many foods where herbs add flavor and also send forth an appetizing fragrance.

Turnips with Sour Cream

3 cups turnips, peeled, boiled, and thinly sliced	1 teaspoon salt
¼ cup thinly sliced celery	½ teaspoon ground coriander
¼ cup diced green pepper	1 onion, chopped
½ cup whole kernel corn, fresh, canned, or frozen	1 apple, sliced
	¼ cup sour cream
	1 tablespoon prepared mustard

Mix all together except the sour cream and mustard. Simmer in a little water until vegetables and apple are soft. Add cream and mustard and bring to a boil.

Rice Pudding

Before I give you my recipe for rice pudding, I am going to tell you how my mother used to make it. She lived on a farm where rich milk was ever ready for her to use. This is her recipe as I wrote it in *Mama's Kitchen,* a book of memories and recipes prepared for my children. "Mama stirred half a cup of sugar and half a cup of rice into two quarts of rich, scalded, fresh whole milk, added a teaspoon of salt, poured this into a greased baking dish, sprinkled the top with cinnamon and baked it slowly, stirring once in awhile, until the milk was absorbed. This took two or three hours. Sometimes she added a handful of raisins before baking it." And now here is my recipe:

3 tablespoons rice	¼ teaspoon ground coriander
2 cups scalded milk	A pinch of salt
¼ cup sugar	

Mix all thoroughly in a quart (or slightly larger) casserole and bake for 2 or 3 hours at 300 F. When most of the milk has been absorbed, the rice should be soft and the pudding slightly brown.

Carrot Pineapple Pudding

1 cup carrots	2 tablespoons soft margarine
¼ cup sugar	3 egg yolks
¼ cup flour	½ cup pineapple juice
½ cup powdered milk	1 cup water
½ teaspoon salt	½ cup crushed pineapple
1 teaspoon ground coriander	3 egg whites

Scrape carrots, slice, cook until tender; drain and blend, sieve, or mash. Thoroughly mix sugar, flour, dried milk, salt, and coriander. Blend in margarine, then egg yolks, next pineapple juice and water, then carrots and pineapple. Beat egg whites until soft peaks form; stir into the carrot mixture; pour into greased casserole; bake at 325 F. until firm, about 40–60 minutes. Serve warm or cold.

Cherry Cake

½ cup margarine	1 teaspoon soda
1 cup sugar	1 teaspoon baking powder
2 eggs	½ teaspoon salt
3 tablespoons sour cream OR sour milk	1 teaspoon ground coriander
2 cups flour	1 cup sour, red, pitted cherries with their juice

Cream margarine and sugar until well blended. Add eggs and beat well; stir in sour cream. Sift together flour, soda, baking powder, salt, and coriander. Add, a third at a time to sugar-egg mixture, stirring after each addition until smooth. Add cherries and mix well.

Pour into greased 8-inch square pan and bake at 350 F. about 30 minutes.

Peanut Butter Cookies

⅞ cup shortening
1 cup brown sugar, firmly packed
½ cup granulated sugar
½ cup crunchy (or smooth) peanut butter
2 eggs, beaten until light and fluffy
2 cups flour

1 teaspoon soda
½ teaspoon baking powder
½ teaspoon salt
2 cups quick-cooking rolled oats
1 teaspoon ground coriander
1 cup raisins simmered in water several minutes, cooled and drained

Cream shortening, sugars, and peanut butter thoroughly. Add eggs. Sift together flour, soda, baking powder, and salt. Add to egg mixture. Add rolled oats, coriander, and raisins. Drop on ungreased cookie sheet and bake at 350 F. This is Gay Anderson Mahshi's recipe.

Green Tomato Mince Pie

When a killing frost seemed just around the corner, we would pick firm green tomatoes, wrap them in newspaper, and store them in a cool place to ripen. We often had them for salads after Thanksgiving. But I always wanted some right away for a mince pie.

1 pint green tomatoes
1 package (9-ounce) mincemeat
1½ cups hot water

¼ cup sugar
1 teaspoon ground coriander

Dice tomatoes; break mincemeat into small chunks; combine the two and add hot water. Cook over low heat until it thickens, about 30 minutes, stirring often to prevent sticking. Add sugar and coriander; pour into pastry-lined pie pan; cover with upper crust. Bake 10 minutes at 425 F. and 30 minutes at 325 F.

Variations: Canned mincemeat may be used instead of packaged, omitting the water. Or it can be made without mincemeat, using finely diced cooked beef, cooking tomatoes and beef with cider, sweetening and seasoning to taste. Molasses or brown sugar can be substituted for white sugar. Use other spices instead of coriander; cardamom, nutmeg, allspice, mace, or a combination of several of these are good.

Carrot Cream Pie

2 cups sliced carrots	¾ cup brown sugar
1 cup water	1 tablespoon soft margarine
½ teaspoon salt	3 egg yolks
⅓ cup cornstarch	1 teaspoon ground coriander
1 cup evaporated milk	

Crust

Use recipe for Graham Cracker Pie Crust (Poppy Seed), but in place of poppy seed add ⅛ teaspoon ground coriander.

Meringue

3 egg whites	⅛ teaspoon ground coriander or
3 tablespoons sugar	just a pinch
⅛ teaspoon salt	
⅛ teaspoon cream of tartar (optional)	

Scrape carrots before slicing; boil with water and salt until carrots are soft, 20−30 minutes. Blend carrots, cornstarch and milk (or sieve or strain carrots and combine with cornstarch and milk). Cream sugar and margarine; stir in egg yolks and coriander. Combine both mixtures; pour into graham cracker crust. Bake 35 minutes at 375 F., or until a toothpick dipped into the filling comes out clean. Remove from oven; turn oven temperature down to 325 F. Prepare meringue by beating egg whites until peaks form; add salt, cream of tartar, and coriander; continue beating, adding sugar a tablespoonful at a time, until sugar is dissolved and meringue is stiff and glossy. Spoon over top of pie; bake until nicely browned 12−15 minutes at 325 F.

Variations: Instead of coriander, use cardamom, same amount; or vanilla, 1 teaspoon for filling, ½ teaspoon for meringue; or ½ teaspoon cinnamon or nutmeg for filling, ¼ teaspoon for meringue. Cream of tartar can be omitted, but it gives a stiffer meringue. Fresh or powdered milk can be substituted for evaporated milk. An unbaked pie shell can be used instead of the graham cracker crust.

Tomato Preserves

1 quart yellow pear tomatoes	2 teaspoons ground ginger OR
4 cups sugar	1 ounce preserved ginger
1 lemon, thinly sliced	1 teaspoon salt
1 tablespoon whole coriander	

Scald and peel the tomatoes; put in large mixing bowl; add sugar; cover and let stand overnight or 8–10 hours. Pour off accumulated syrup and boil gently half an hour. Slice lemon as thinly as possible, discarding the seeds. Add lemon, tomatoes, coriander, ginger, and salt to the syrup. Simmer about 3 hours, until tomatoes look clear and syrup is thick. Stir occasionally at first, more frequently as it thickens. Pour into sterilized jars and seal with paraffin.

Variations: Red cherry tomatoes or quartered large yellow or red tomatoes can be used.

Comfits

Comfits, or candied seeds and nuts, can be made with coriander seeds. Candied coriander is popular in some countries and is used as a breath sweetener. Dip seeds in slightly beaten egg white and then in granulated sugar. Spread on waxed paper to dry.

A Coriander Drink

I have made a very refreshing drink by pouring a cup of boiling water over ¼ teaspoonful of ground coriander and 1 teaspoonful of sugar.

See also Cherry Molasses Cake (Cardamom), Coffee (Cardamom), Cottage Cheese Plus (Cardamom), Pineapple Cottage Cheese Dessert (Cardamom), Whole Wheat Bread (Sesame); *and* Herb Honey, Herb Vinegar.

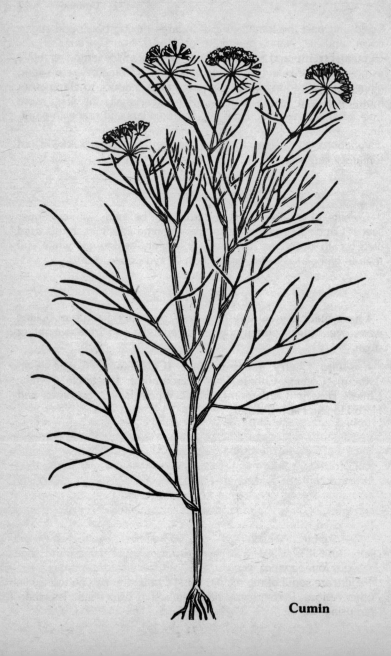

Cumin

Cumin *Cuminum cyminum*

Cumin is not as well known in the United States as it is in many other countries. This is a shame for it has a distinctive flavor, pleasing to many. The first time I used it was in a lamb stew which I served to friends who had just been skiing on a crisp winter day. I was astonished at the enthusiasm of one guest who had grown up in India. He said that it was his first taste of cumin since he left India, where as a boy he had learned to like it, especially in meat dishes. In Mexico, known as *comino,* it is considered indispensible for such dishes as chili con carne and tamales. In France it is an ingredient in some fine soups. Germans use it in sauerkraut. Scandinavian cooks appreciate its warm, slightly bitter taste in their baking. It is probably the best liked of all spices in Arab countries. It was a tithing herb in biblical times. It was reported to be used by some medieval students, who believed it would make them look pale and learned like their professor. The seeds, chewed, were supposed to remove the smell of onions from one's breath; perhaps they still do. Cumin was once thought to have medical uses. Banckes's *Herbal,* printed in 1525, has this to say of cumin, "It's virtue is to destroy wicked winds and other evils in man's stomach."

Cumin, like caraway, dill, and many other useful herbs, belongs to the Umbelliferae or parsley family. Unlike some of them, it is a rather untidy looking plant, a 4–8-inch tall annual with threadlike leaves and dull white or pinkish flowers. The seeds, whole or ground, are available in many grocery and health stores. You may like them for occasional use as well as I do. Try them scattered on sugar cookies, in rye bread, cottage cheese or deviled eggs, meat loaf or other ground-meat dishes, lamb or beef stews, in the water in which cabbage and other strong-flavored vegetables are cooked. You may like to use it as a substitute for caraway or pepper. A sprinkling of ground cumin in a cup of hot water might still "destroy the wicked winds."

Cumin, in the Middle Ages, was considered a symbol of miserliness. Use it now like a miser—¼ teaspoon of the ground seeds seasons four servings, but you may soon like a little more.

Here are some of my recipes using cumin; I hope you will try it in other recipes. Perhaps you had better start with a little less than I am using.

Chicken Vegetable Soup

¼ cup diced onion
¼ cup diced celery
¼ cup diced carrot
½ cup cooked, diced chicken

4 cups chicken broth
½ cup noodles
¼ teaspoon cumin

Add vegetables and chicken with noodles and cumin to boiling broth and cook until done, about 20 minutes. Salt to taste if broth is not already salted.

Variations: Other vegetables and herbs can be substituted or added (*see* Lamb Stew *under* Leek).

Bunny's Casserole

1 small onion, minced
1 pound hamburger
1 can cream of mushroom soup
1 can of water
¼ cup soy sauce

1 cup chopped celery
½ cup uncooked rice
¼ teaspoon cumin
1 can Chinese noodles

Fry onion and hamburger together; pour off any excess fat. Stir mushroom soup, water, and soy sauce together. Add this and celery, rice, and cumin to hamburger. Mix well, pour into casserole, cover, and bake 1 hour at 350 F. Remove cover, sprinkle with noodles and bake 15 minutes more. My niece, Bunny Zuidmeer, gave me this recipe; I added cumin.

Variations: Crushed corn flakes or granola instead of Chinese noodles are also good toppings.

A Corn Bread Dinner

1 cup yellow cornmeal
1¼ cup buttermilk
1 cup grated cheese
1 cup finely sliced celery
1 cup flour
2 teaspoons baking powder

1 teaspoon soda
1 teaspoon salt
½ teaspoon cumin
2 eggs
¼ cup cooking oil

Put cornmeal into large mixing bowl; add buttermilk and let soak while preparing the other ingredients. Grate cheese and slice celery; put flour, baking powder, soda, salt, and cumin into the flour sifter. Now add eggs and oil to cornmeal, stir briskly; continue stirring while sifting in dry ingredients. Stir in celery and cheese. Pour into greased pan and bake 30 minutes (or until done) at 375 F. This corn bread is good simply buttered and better yet when split, put in a soup bowl, and served with meat gravy, cream sauce, or with a cream soup (mushroom, cheese, onion, or celery) which has been diluted with half a can of water or milk and heated.

Variations: Instead of cheese, a 7-ounce can of corned beef can be added before baking, or two frankfurters in quarter-inch slices. Powdered reconstituted buttermilk can be used instead of fresh. Or use fresh or reconstituted milk instead of buttermilk, substituting another teaspoon of baking powder for the soda. With fruit for dessert and a hot drink this makes a complete meal—carbohydrates, protein, vegetables.

Rice

1 cup rice (white or brown)	1 teaspoon whole cumin seeds
3 cups cold water	OR ¼ teaspoon ground
1 teaspoon salt	cumin seeds
1 tablespoon margarine or butter	

Bring rice and water to a boil. Add salt, margarine, and cumin seeds. If whole seeds are used, tie them in a muslin bag and remove before serving. Reduce heat and simmer 45 minutes (less for white rice). Serve with meat sauce or cream of mushroom soup (dilute the soup with ½ can water). Serves four.

Cumined Vegetables

1 cup peeled and sliced turnips	½ cup cream of mushroom soup
½ cup thinly sliced celery	¼ cup water
¼ cup diced green pepper	½ cup buttered bread crumbs
¼ cup diced onion	¼ cup grated cheese
½ cup whole kernel corn	
1 teaspoon salt	
1 teaspoon cumin seed	
½ cup water	

Mix first 8 ingredients well and simmer until almost soft—about 15 minutes if vegetables are not too old. Combine soup and water; add to vegetables and stir; put in casserole; top with bread crumbs and cheese. Bake at 400 F. until nicely browned, about 15 minutes.

Spice for Indian Curry

This recipe was given me by Hazel Hauck, a home economics teacher who worked on the diet of natives in India and Africa. She said that many different combinations of spices were used in those countries and that Americans could improve their cooking by making their own combinations for curry. She suggested pre-assembling the following three different combinations for use with meat, vegetables, rice, or other foods that combine with curry. One-half to 1 teaspoon is recommended for 1 quart of food. Start with a little and next time add more depending upon personal taste.

1 tablespoon plus 1 teaspoon cumin and coriander in equal portions
1 tablespoon mustard seed and 1¼ tablespoons caraway and a few whole black peppers
1 teaspoon ground cloves and 1 teaspoon ground cardamom

Cumin Seed Wafers

¾ cup margarine   2 cups sifted flour
1 cup grated cheese   ½ teaspoon salt
1 teaspoon cumin

Cream margarine, cheese, and cumin. Sift in flour and salt. Form into 1½-inch rolls. Wrap in waxed paper or foil. Chill several hours or overnight in refrigerator. Slice thin. Bake on ungreased cookie sheet at 400 F. 10 minutes or until lightly browned. Serve hot or cold.

See also Apple Pie (Anise), Coffee (Cardamom), Lamb Stew (Leek), Onion Pie (Caraway), Scrambled Eggs (Basil).

Dill *Anethum graveolens*

Dill, a biennial member of the Umbelliferae (parsley or carrot family), is usually grown as an annual. Late in summer it is in much demand for seasoning dill pickles. The lacy, finely divided leaves and the clusters of small yellow flowers add a delicate touch to bouquets. Throughout the centuries dill has had many other uses. Wreaths of the flowers crowned Roman and Grecian heroes. Dill leaves and flowers were strewn on banquet floors, where their penetrating fragrance seemed to cleanse the heavy air. Dill warded off (so it was claimed) the evils of witchcraft. It was also considered a lucky omen—in Flanders, a bride pinned sprigs of dill on her wedding dress, hoping to ensure a happy married life. In our country pioneer mothers took a handful of dill seeds to church, chewing them to relieve the tedium of long sermons, and distributing them to quiet small children; they were supposed to have a sedative value—the name dill is said to come from a Norse word, *dilla,* meaning to lull. I have read that dill-seed sweetmeats are still liked in India.

I have also read that dill as an herb is almost as well known in the United States as sage or parsley. That may well be true, for it is a valuable herb with many uses. First of all, we know it best as a seasoning for one of our most popular pickles. The aromatic oil that makes it so good in pickles also gives it value in salads and other vegetable dishes. It softens the taste of beets, cabbage, and strong-flavored vegetables; gives zest to milder ones. It is good with fish (try it with chicken); good with rice (try it with macaroni); good with apples (try it with pears and prunes).

To serve four it is suggested that you use ⅛ to ½ teaspoon of ground seed or ½ to 2 teaspoons of whole seed—use the lesser amounts until you are sure you like the flavor. Two tablespoons of chopped fresh leaves are good in salads, or wherever you want them, and instead of parsley, for a garnish. One small leafy sprig (called dill weed) can be added to soups, stews, vegetables, and other cooked foods. I like to add a tablespoon of dill vinegar to the water in which I poach eggs or fish.

Here are a few of my favorite recipes using dill. Of course I sometimes add it to other recipes or use other herbs in these recipes.

Dill

Mrs. Bender's Dill Pickles

I took this recipe east with me when we went from Lynden, Washington, to Ithaca, New York, where my husband, just released from service in World War I, returned to finish his graduate work at Cornell University. He stayed on at Cornell to teach. Perhaps because this recipe reminded me of Lynden, I marked it "Best" for pickles but probably also because it was simple and good.

1 quart vinegar	Dill, 1½ tablespoons seed OR a few
3 quarts water	sprigs (leaves, flowers, and seeds)
1 cup salt	20–25 whole cucumbers
Grape leaves	

Mix vinegar, water, and salt and boil 5 minutes. Put a grape leaf and dill to cover bottom of sterilized quart jar. Pack full of cucumbers (that have been washed and soaked in weak brine overnight); put grape leaf and dill to cover on top; fill jar with hot liquid; seal tightly.

Some years later Gil Dobie gave me a recipe for dill pickles. He was also from Washington and at that time head football coach at Cornell University. He brought excellent, crisp, tasty dill pickles to a picnic of the Northwestern Club.

Gil Dobie's Dill Pickles

This is a large recipe; I make it up using one-half or one-fourth of the ingredients. I do not always add red pepper, mustard seed, or horseradish root.

½ cup salt	Dill, 2 or 3 sprigs for each jar
4 quarts water	Red pepper (optional)
100 medium-sized cucumbers	1 cup mustard seed (optional)
10 quarts water	1 cup horseradish root, shaved
1 quart vinegar	fine (optional)
2 cups salt	

Make a brine by adding ½ cup salt to 4 quarts of water; in this soak the cucumbers overnight. Be sure brine covers cucumbers. The same evening boil together 10 quarts water, 1 quart vinegar, 2 cups salt; let this brine stand overnight. In the morning drain cucumbers and pack tight in 2-quart sterilized jars with dill. Add a small piece red pepper to each jar. Bring second brine to a boil; pour over cucumbers; seal jars.

Variations: One cup mustard seed and 1 cup horseradish root may be added before sealing, dividing among jars.

Tomato Juice with Dill

1 quart tomato juice
1 teaspoon dill seed OR 1 tablespoon fresh dill weed

Bring tomato juice and dill to a boil; let stand 1 hour or longer. Serve iced or reheated.

Dill and Cottage Cheese Salad

2 teaspoons dill weed
2 tablespoons salad dressing OR mayonnaise
½ cup grated carrot
½ cup shredded lettuce
1 tablespoon minced or grated onion
1 cup cottage cheese

Blend dill and dressing and let stand 1−2 hours. Toss other ingredients together and lightly stir in dressing.

Dill Tossed Salad

2 cups lettuce, bite-sized
½ cup shredded carrot
½ cup diced celery
1 tomato, diced
1 tablespoon diced onion (optional)
⅛ teaspoon dill seed
Mayonnaise to moisten

Mix and toss all ingredients and add mayonnaise at the last minute.
Variation: Instead of mayonnaise, use the Healthful Salad Dressing (*below*).

Healthful Salad Dressing
Juice ½ lemon
1 tablespoon salad oil
Few grains of salt

Mix and add to tossed salad just before serving.

Dill Vinegar

Dill vinegar, made by soaking the seed or the foliage and flowers in vinegar, is a good dressing for cabbage and other vegetables, either when served as a salad or when cooked. (*See* Herb Vinegar.)

Dill Sauce

2 tablespoons margarine
2 tablespoons flour
½ teaspoon salt

1 teaspoon dill weed OR ½ teaspoon dill seed
1 cup milk

Melt margarine over low heat and stir in flour. Add salt, dill and milk; slowly bring to a boil, stirring all the time, and cook until thickened (about 5 minutes), stirring occasionally. Serve over rice, noodles, macaroni, or boiled potatoes. Also good over fish.

Apple Crisp with Dill

2 cups finely sliced apples
1 teaspoon dill seed
¼ cup margarine
1 egg

¾ cup sugar
¾ cup flour
2 teaspoons baking powder
½ teaspoon salt

Place apples in greased casserole and sprinkle with dill seed. To make batter, blend margarine and egg, sift in dry ingredients, and stir until well mixed. Drop by teaspoonfuls on apples. Bake 40 minutes at 350 F. Serve warm with cream or vanilla ice cream.

Variations: Use fennel or fenugreek in place of dill.

Dill Tea

1 teaspoon dill seed

2 cups cold water

Bring dill and water to a boil, reduce heat, and simmer 5 minutes. Serve with or without sugar or lemon, but usually without milk or cream. A warming and refreshing drink for a winter afternoon.

See also Easiest Fried Chicken (Rosemary), Herbed Beets (Anise), Potato Salad (Sorrel), Scrambled Eggs (Basil), Sour Cream Sauce (Horseradish).

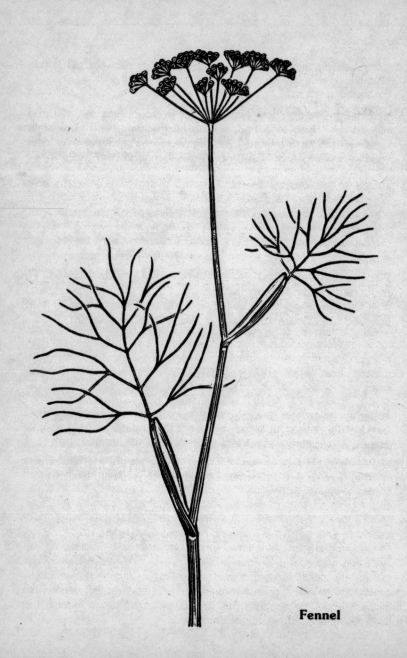

Fennel

Fennel *Foeniculum vulgare*

This perennial member of the parsley or Umbelliferae family can be an attractive addition to the flower bed, especially if placed at the back. Its tall stems (4 or 5 feet) have lacy leaves and clusters of umbels of small yellow flowers. All parts of the plant have an anise or caraway flavor. I like to chew a few leaves while working in the garden. I also like to add clusters of flowers or of young seeds to bouquets.

Modern science is finding a basis of truth in some of the old superstitions. I wonder about this one—centuries ago fennel was supposed to be a reducer's joy. In 1657, Wm. Coles advised using fennel in drinks or broth "for those that are grown fat to abate their unwieldiness and cause them to grow more gaunt and lank." He was not the first to give this advice—in 1585, a Mr. Dawson published a recipe for a slenderizing tea made with fennel seed. Drinking fennel was also supposed to be good for the eyes. Sprigs of fennel symbolized flattery and were an emblem of heroism. In our own colonial days fennel seeds went to church; coated with sugar they were one of the "meetin' house seeds" that quieted restless children and kept their parents awake during the long sermons.

Today the seeds, flavoring a bedtime drink of warm milk, can help us when sleep is slow in coming. Steeped with our morning coffee (especially appreciated in coffee substitutes), they can help us welcome the day. They also add to the relaxing pleasure of an afternoon teatime break. The seeds are used in cakes, cookies, and bread; they can be added to apple desserts, to certain vegetables, and to fish and meat dishes. The leaves, fresh or dried, are also good for seasoning these dishes; fresh leaves are especially good in salads or as a garnish for soups.

Two varieties are sometimes grown in vegetable gardens; if you are lucky you may find them in food stores. Florence fennel, more commonly called finocchio, has an enlarged and thickened base which can be eaten raw or cooked and served as a root vegetable. Sicilian fennel or caroselle has larger thickened stems, which are used like celery, either raw or cooked.

I frequently find a new use for fennel in the kitchen; this is true of all the culinary herbs. I hope the following recipes will give you an idea of the varied uses of fennel and will suggest other recipes in which to try this piquant herb.

Zucchini Bread

3 well-beaten eggs
1½ cups sugar
¾ cup oil
3 cups flour
1 teaspoon salt
½ teaspoon soda

1 teaspoon baking powder
1 teaspoon nutmeg
2 cups grated zucchini
½ cup chopped nuts
1 teaspoon fennel seed

Beat eggs, stir in sugar, then oil. Sift flour, salt, soda, baking powder, and nutmeg together. Add to eggs, sugar, and oil. Add grated zucchini, nuts, and fennel; stir until well mixed. Spoon into 2 large pans (or a number of small ones) and bake at 350 F. until done, 40 minutes to 1 hour. Test with a cake tester or toothpick to be sure it is done. Remove from pans a few minutes after taking loaves from oven.

Note: If squash is old and hard-shelled, peel before grating, but peeling is not necessary with tender young squash.

Salmon Casserole

1 tablespoon margarine
2 tablespoons flour
1 cup milk
¼ teaspoon salt
¼ teaspoon fennel seed
1-pound can salmon

1 cup bread or cracker crumbs
¼ cup grated cheese
1 tablespoon minced green pepper (optional)
1 tablespoon minced onion (optional)

Make a white sauce by melting margarine, blending in flour, and adding milk slowly. Cook over low heat, stirring constantly until thickened. Add salt and fennel seed. Remove from heat; stir in salmon and ¾ cup of the bread or cracker crumbs. Pour into casserole, sprinkle with cheese and remaining ¼ cup crumbs. Bake 30 minutes at 350 F. Green pepper and/or onion can be added with salmon to white sauce.

Meatballs with Gravy

Meatballs
- 1 tablespoon margarine or oil
- 1 cup ground meat
- ¼ cup cracker crumbs
- 2 tablespoons milk
- ½ teaspoon salt
- ¼ teaspoon fennel seed

Gravy
- 2 tablespoons fat
- 3 tablespoons flour
- 2 cups water
- ¼ teaspoon salt
- Pinch fennel seeds

Melt margarine in a heavy skillet; thoroughly mix other ingredients; form into small balls (about 1 rounded teaspoonful to a ball—larger if you wish); sauté in margarine or oil, turning so all sides are browned. Add a little boiling water and cook 10 minutes—longer if balls are larger. Remove meatballs from pan; pour off fat; measure 2 tablespoons of fat and return it to the skillet. To this fat add flour and cook over low heat, stirring constantly until it is as brown as you like. Remove from heat; slowly stir in water; return to heat and add salt, fennel seed, and meatballs. Cook 2 minutes after it begins to boil, stirring several times while it is heating. These meatballs are good for lunch or supper, with salad; equally good over toast, potatoes, corn bread, macaroni, or noodles.

Cabbage Casserole

- 3 cups chopped cabbage
- ¼ cup sliced onions
- ½ teaspoon salt
- ½ cup water
- ½ cup cream of mushroom soup
- ¼ cup grated cheese
- ¼ teaspoon fennel
- ½ cup finely crumbled dry bread crumbs

Cook cabbage and onion in salted boiling water until wilted (not more than 5 minutes). Drain, stir in soup, and pour into greased casserole. Top with bread crumbs, cheese, and fennel, which have been well mixed together. Bake at 350 F. until browned, 20–30 minutes.

Variations: Other vegetables can be used instead of cabbage, such as snap beans, summer squash, or turnips. Almost any culinary herb could be substituted for fennel. Other cream soups or thick cream sauce could take the place of mushroom soup. If cream-of-cheese soup is used, omit cheese from topping.

Rutabagas Plus

2 cups rutabagas, diced and   ¼ cup diced green pepper
  cooked   ½ cup sliced celery
¼ cup sliced tomatoes   ½ cup water
¼ cup diced onion   ½ teaspoon fennel seed

Combine ingredients and bring to a boil. Drop dumplings (*see below*), a teaspoonful at a time on vegetables. Cover and cook 10 minutes. Serve immediately.

Dumplings

¾ cup self-rising flour   ½ cup milk
1 tablespoon oil

Mix all ingredients lightly and drop onto vegetables. Instead of self-rising flour, use ¾ cup flour, sifted with 1 teaspoon baking powder and ½ teaspoon salt.

A Bedtime Drink

1 cup cold milk   ⅛ teaspoon fennel seeds

Over low heat, steep the milk and fennel until milk is lukewarm. Drink slowly just before retiring.

See also Apple Crisp with Dill, Chocolate Chip Cookies (Poppy Seed), Herbed Beets (Anise), Herb Seed Cookies (Sesame), Pot Roast with Thyme, Swedish Limpa (Caraway), Thyme in an Oven Roast; *and* Herb Honey.

Fenugreek

Fenugreek *Trigonella foenum-graecum*

If you have never heard of fenugreek, I am not surprised. I had not either until the day I saw it on the herb and spice shelf of the Cooperative Consumers store in Ithaca, New York. Many groceries do not yet carry it, but you should be able to find it in a health food or organic food store. There were many kinds of herb seeds on that shelf and many I knew nothing about. I decided that probably many other persons were as ignorant of their uses as I was, so I bought every kind they had, took them home, smelled and tasted them, made up recipes for their use, and was glad that I had these new seasonings.

As I left that day with my assortment of herb seeds, I met an elderly friend who I knew was knowledgeable about good health as affected by good nutrition. I asked him what I could do with fenugreek, and he instantly answered, "Tea, of course." That evening I learned why he was so enthusiastic about it. Later that winter I learned that fenugreek can give a fine flavor to meat dishes. It is also good with the stronger flavored vegetables, with gingerbread, and with fruit pies and puddings.

Fenugreek is an annual belonging to the Leguminosae or pea family. It is seldom seen in American gardens, but with the increasing interest in nutrition, it may soon be grown for greens and salads. In India and Egypt, perhaps in other countries too, fenugreek is grown, and the young plants are eaten raw or cooked. Fenugreek seeds are an essential ingredient in some curry mixtures. The seeds have a slightly maplelike taste; the leaves and stems more like celery. The seed pods are long, slim, and remind one of string beans.

Fenugreek, because of its real or imagined medicinal properties, was one of the herbs in the Physic Gardens of monasteries a thousand years ago. It is claimed that, taken at bedtime, it will induce restful sleep, but do not make too strong a tea. I know that it is pleasant to drink at bedtime or any time.

Pork Pie with Corn Bread Topping

2 cups diced cooked pork
1 package frozen mixed vegetables

1 can chicken gravy
½ cup water
1 teaspoon fenugreek seed

86

Combine all ingredients and stir well; bring to a boil. Pour into baking dish. Spoon on corn bread topping (*below*) and bake at 375 F. 30 minutes. Serves 6.

Variations: Gravy from the roast can be used instead of chicken gravy. Basil can be substituted for the fenugreek, about 1 teaspoon.

Corn Bread Topping

¾ cup yellow cornmeal	½ cup flour
¾ cup buttermilk	1 teaspoon salt
1 egg, beaten	¾ teaspoon soda
2 tablespoons vegetable oil	

Soak cornmeal in buttermilk 5 minutes. Add egg and oil. Sift in other ingredients and mix. Spoon over top of pie.

Another Meat Sauce

1 tablespoon bacon fat	1 can tomato sauce with cheese
1 pound hamburger	1 tablespoon dried minced onion
1 can water	1 teaspoon fenugreek seed

Melt fat in skillet, add hamburger, and cook, stirring until no longer pink. Drain off excess fat; add remaining ingredients; cook slowly 30 minutes to 1 hour or longer—the longer the better.

Variations: Margarine, oil, or other fat can be used instead of bacon fat, 3 tablespoons diced onion instead of dried onion, and grated cheese on top just before serving. If grated cheese is added, use regular tomato sauce or a can of stewed tomatoes.

Carrot Casserole

2 cups sliced carrots	1 teaspoon fenugreek seed
1 cup boiling water	1 tablespoon brown sugar
¾ teaspoon salt	2 tablespoons margarine
3 tablespoons frozen orange juice concentrate	⅓ cup grated cheese
	¾ cup bread crumbs
½ cup water	

Scrape and slice carrots; cook with the cup of boiling salted water 10 minutes; drain and pour into greased casserole. Mix orange concentrate, water, fenugreek seed, and sugar; pour over carrots. Melt margarine; stir in bread crumbs; sprinkle on top of carrots; and sprinkle cheese over bread. Bake at 350 F. 20–30 minutes, until bubbly and lightly browned.

Peanut Butter Apple Quickie

2½ cups sliced apples
⅓ cup honey
⅓ cup peanut butter
1 tablespoon oil
1 egg

½ cup flour
½ cup quick cooking oats
2 tablespoons baking powder
½ teaspoon salt
½ teaspoon fenugreek seed

Arrange apples in 10-x-6-inch baking dish. Mix all other ingredients and crumble over apples. Bake uncovered 40–50 minutes at 350 F. until nicely browned. Serve warm or cold, plain, with cream, or topped with vanilla ice cream.

Fenugreek Tea

¼ teaspoon fenugreek seed,
    more if you wish

1 cup cold water
1 teaspoon honey (optional)

Bring fenugreek seed and water to a boil; steep for 5 minutes. Strain; add honey if desired (or sugar). Sip slowly; sleep well!

See also Apple Crisp with Dill, Apple Pie (Anise), Lamb Stew (Leek).

Garlic   *Allium sativum*

Garlic has for centuries been a favored seasoning in many countries and is now becoming increasingly popular in America. It is a perennial member of the lily family; its grey-green leaves and its white to pinkish flowers are ornamental wherever grown but it is even more welcome in the herb or vegetable garden than in the flower bed. Like many other herbs, garlic has been called the miracle herb and was thought to have magic powers. Roman soldiers ate garlic for courage in battle; bullfighters because a bull was supposed not to charge the matador if he smelled of it; athletes to give them strength; the Israelites in their long journey through the deserts of Arabia looked back longingly to the garlic they had previously enjoyed. The medicinal value of garlic was long ago recognized. To quote from a writer in the 17th century, "Our apothecary shop is a garden full of herbs, our doctor a clove of garlic." It is claimed that if you regularly eat enough garlic your system will assimilate it and your breath will not smell, also that if you chew parsley after eating garlic your breath will not be offensive.

If you can raise your own garlic, you are lucky, for it is stronger and better than any you buy. It is a perennial, best if harvested when the leaves have yellowed and dried. It should be stored in a cool place for winter use, saving a few bulbs to divide and plant early in the spring. If you do not have an outdoor garden, you might try planting a few cloves (the small bulblets that constitute a garlic bulb) in a pot for your kitchen window-sill garden. If you are not raising your own garlic, many groceries sell the dried bulbs or products made from them. You may find garlic chips or powder, salt, oil, and vinegar. All are good; all should be used, but not too generously. Here are a couple quotes for garlic lovers: "Garlic has an extraordinary capacity for blending and accenting the other ingredients without revealing its own identity"; and the reason Italian cookery is so good is because it has "a delicate and undetected flavor of garlic."

Garlic cloves are easier to peel if boiled for 3 to 4 minutes; they are also easier then to crush. If you have not used garlic, you might try substituting it for onions, but use it sparingly until you learn just how much you and your family will enjoy. Last night I tried it in scalloped potatoes. I wish that I had done so years ago.

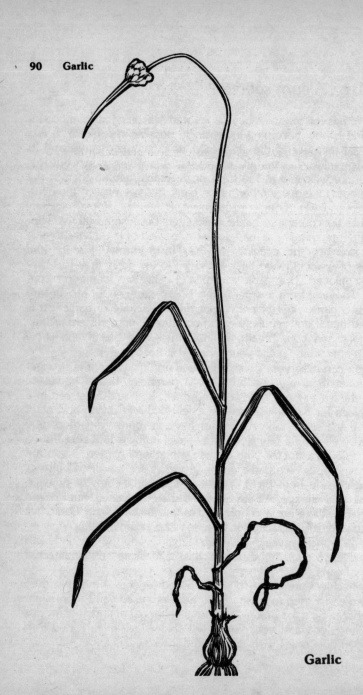

Garlic

Scalloped Potatoes

2 cups thinly sliced potatoes	½ cup rich milk
1 tablespoon garlic cloves	½ teaspoon salt
1 tablespoon margarine	Parsley or chervil (optional)

Slice peeled garlic cloves as thin as possible and crush them; melt the margarine over low heat, add the garlic, and cook for a few minutes, stirring frequently. Heat milk; add salt, margarine-garlic, and parsley or chervil; pour over potatoes in casserole; and bake until tender, 30−40 minutes at 350 F. Half this amount makes a single serving; recipe can be doubled or more.

Garlic Butter

1 teaspoon garlic powder OR 1 tablespoon—or less—garlic	½ cup (1 stick) margarine 1 teaspoon lemon juice

If fresh garlic is used, it should be peeled, finely sliced, and well crushed (a garlic press is great for this). Cream margarine, add lemon juice and garlic, and blend well. Let stand 1 hour or more at room temperature. Store in covered jar and keep in refrigerator.

Garlic Bread

French bread is fine for this but any bread can be used; you should have a medium-sized unsliced loaf. Cut fairly thick slices almost to the lower crust. Spread with garlic butter, wrap loaf in foil; heat 20−25 minutes at 425 F. Or completely slice the bread; place the buttered (margarined) slices on a cookie sheet and toast at 400 F. until nicely browned, about 6 minutes. Instead of spreading with garlic butter, I sometimes spread with margarine and then sprinkle with powdered garlic.

Garlic Vinegar

1 tablespoon garlic cloves	1 pint vinegar

Slice garlic cloves; they do not need to be peeled. Heat vinegar but do not boil. Pour vinegar over garlic in jar that can be sealed. Seal and let stand for two weeks in a warm room. Shake every few days. Strain and pour into sterile bottles. If garlic vinegar is wanted sooner, use more cloves of garlic.

Chicken with Pineapple

3-pound chicken, cut into serving
   pieces
1 cup pineapple chunks, canned
   or frozen, well drained
¾ cup pineapple juice
1 teaspoon ground ginger

2 tablespoons soy sauce
2 cloves garlic, finely cut and
   crushed
¼ cup cooking oil or melted
   margarine

Make a marinade of everything except chicken and oil. Pour over the chicken and let stand in refrigerator several hours (best of all overnight); turn the pieces a time or two. Drain the chicken and brown in oil. Put chicken in casserole; pour on marinade; bake until tender, 45 minutes to 1 hour, at 325 F. Do not cover casserole. Baste several times while baking with marinade from pan.

Variations: One cup of drained crushed pineapple can be substituted for the pineapple chunks. One tablespoon finely cut preserved ginger or freshly grated ginger root can be used instead of the powdered ginger. Soy sauce may be omitted.

Friends often share their recipes with me. Here are two worth recommending. The first comes from Carol DeCabrera in Lima, Peru; the second from Hildegard Dietze, a neighbor of mine. The love of garlic knows no national boundaries.

Baked Fish

Cut the fish in halves; rub both sides with a paste made from garlic and pepper; put in greased pan or casserole; add 1 tablespoon soy sauce and bake at 350 F. 'til tender and flakey, about 30 minutes. Quite unusual.

Garlic Sauce for Spaghetti or Other Pasta

Slice thinly 8–12 peeled cloves of garlic. Sauté gently at low temperature in a mixture of ½ cup olive oil and butter. Remove from heat and slowly add ¼ cup hot water. Return to stove and simmer 5 minutes with cover on pan. Add salt and pepper to taste. Pour over pasta and toss lightly with Romano cheese.

Garlic with Lamb and Pork

Another neighbor says that garlic is indispensable with lamb and just as good with pork.

Garlic in Salads

I suppose if you really like garlic you would want to slice one or more (depending upon the size of the salad and how much garlic flavor you want) peeled cloves of garlic and add to other ingredients of a vegetable, fish, meat, or chicken salad. If you want just a touch of garlic, just a suggestion of its flavor, you can rub the salad bowl with a cut garlic clove. Or you may spread a slice of bread with garlic butter, cut it into small cubes, and add this to the salad. Or you can make the salad dressing with garlic vinegar.

See also Egg Sandwich Filling (Shallots), Gazpacho La Quinta (Parsley), Parsley Butter, Pot Roast with Thyme, Thyme in an Oven Roast, Whipped Cream Sauce (Horseradish).

Geranium *Pelargonium*

Geraniums are so much at home in our gardens and our houses that it is hard to realize that they came from the far south—the tip of South Africa. Early in the 17th century Dutch or English sailing vessels brought them to Europe, where they were raised extensively. Not only were they prized for their beauty, they were of great commercial value. It was learned that some varieties had an oil that could be used instead of expensive rose oil in perfumes, soaps, and other toiletries. For this reason geraniums were extensively cultivated, especially in France and Turkey. They were planted in England for their landscape value. In fact, during the 1800's England and the continent enjoyed a geranium craze. It is no wonder, therefore, that by 1750 geraniums were a part of many American gardens.

They are not winter hardy except in the south but are propagated readily by slips, also by seeds. Many varieties have unusually beautiful flowers; others are treasured for the texture, shape, or fragrance of their leaves. The rose geranium has long been recognized as a fine food flavorer; others are also good. Fragrant-leaved geraniums are divided into seven classes: rose, lemon, mint, fruit, nut, spice, and pungent. Over 50 kinds with a rose odor are now grown.

I like to have a rose geranium near my telephone. When a call goes on and on, I like to pinch a leaf and treat myself to its invigorating perfume. A peppermint geranium is equally delightful, as are many of the other fragrant-leaved geraniums. Because of the fragrance released, picking dead leaves from any geranium is one of the most enjoyable garden chores. Because of their fragrance and flavor, geranium leaves are good seasoning for baking, in desserts, and in drinks. Although the rose geranium is usually named in recipes, you can use any of the fragrant-leaved ones interchangeably. I hope that the following recipes will suggest others to you. Just remember not to use too many leaves at a time. How good your home will smell when you are cooking with geraniums!

Mrs. Kenerson's Sponge Cake

You may have read in old cookbooks about putting geranium leaves in the bottom of a cake pan before pouring in the batter. Mrs. Kenerson did not suggest it for the recipe that she gave me over 50 years ago, but it is especially well suited for this. I leave out the lemon extract when flavoring it with rose geranium leaves. Here is her recipe with my addition.

2 eggs, well beaten
1½ scant cups sugar beaten into the eggs
1 scant cup cold water slopped in
2 cups flour, 1½ teaspoons baking powder, a little salt sifted together three times and gradually stirred in

1 teaspoon lemon extract
Rose geranium leaves

Place leaves in bottom of 9-x-12-inch pan, leaving space between them, pour in batter, bake until done, about 30 minutes, at 325 F.

Apricot Tapioca Pudding

¼ cup pearl tapioca
¾ cup cold water
1½ cups milk
¼ teaspoon salt
1 cup apricots and juice, canned or cooked

½ cup sugar
1 peppermint geranium leaf (1 tablespoon)
2 egg yolks
2 egg whites
1 tablespoon sugar

Soak tapioca in water 3–4 hours or overnight. Drain any remaining water; add milk and salt; cook 1 hour in top of double boiler OR bake at 350 F. Blend apricots and juice, geranium leaf, 1½ cups sugar and egg yolks in electric blender until thoroughly mixed. Remove tapioca from stove or oven and very slowly stir apricots into tapioca mixture. Heat again (about 5 minutes). Beat egg whites to soft peaks; add sugar, beating until stiff; fold lightly into pudding and cook another 10 minutes. Serve warm or cold, stirring at least once while it cools. This is good made with fresh milk, reconstituted dry milk, or diluted evaporated milk.

Variation: If you have no blender, cook the geranium leaf with the tapioca in the double boiler or oven and then remove it. Press the apricots and juice through a strainer or sieve, and then mix well with sugar and egg yolks.

Geranium Sugar

1 pound granulated sugar   6–12 geranium leaves

Pour sugar into a screw-top jar, while adding a leaf at regular intervals. Seal and let stand a couple of weeks. Leaves can be removed then or as sugar is used; or they can be crumbled and used with it. This sugar is good in stewed fruit, baked apples, and other desserts, in cakes, cookies, and cake icings, or sprinkled on top of cookies. You may want to dilute the flavor with granulated sugar. The number of leaves used depends upon the strength of fragrance in the leaves—rose geranium, for instance, will need more than peppermint geranium.

Other Uses for Geranium Leaves

Fragrant-leaved geraniums can add flavor to many foods. They can be floated in wine cups, punch bowls, or lemonade, in hot or cold tea, in coffee or cocoa. They can be placed in the bottom of trays or bowls in which ice cream, custards, or gelatin desserts are spooned or in cookie trays or cake pans. *See also* Candied Leaves, Flowers, and Seeds; Herb Jelly; Herb Vinegar.

The usefulness of geranium leaves is not limited to foods. They can add to the pleasure of a hot bath or of rubbing alcohol. They can be a chief ingredient of fragrance bags or of potpourri. Your imagination may add still more uses for these delightfully fragrant leaves. Just brushing against them in the garden or pinching them in the house is a pleasure. *See also* Lemon Verbena.

See also Sugarless Cookies (Cardamom).

Good-King-Henry *Chenopodium bonus-henricus*

This is, I think, my favorite green, although it is almost tied with dandelions. So far as I'm concerned, both are better than spinach. Nobody knows why it is called Good-King-Henry, although a guess is that it was a favorite dish of his. There is no question, however, as to why it is also called wild or perennial spinach. Supposedly it was brought from Europe by our early settlers as a green vegetable. It has a rather mild, slightly bitter taste. Some cooks use it with regular spinach; some add a few leaves to soups; a few add the leaves to salads in the spring. This is the way I like it:

My Favorite Greens

1 quart or more Good-King-Henry	1 tablespoon fat
	1 tablespoon flour
2 tablespoons water	Salt to taste

Pick 2- or 3-inch tender tips from the plants, using both leaves and stems. Wash carefully and put into the cooking pot without shaking off water; add a little water and a very little salt—more can be added later if needed. Cook until somewhat tender, about 10 minutes. With kitchen shears or a knife cut greens into small pieces (sometimes I do as my German mother-in-law did and push them through a sieve), or put them very briefly in a blender. Return this to the stove, add fat, sprinkle on flour, and stir until well mixed; bring to a boil and simmer 5 minutes, stirring constantly.

Variations for this or any greens: A difference in flavor results when you use a different cooking fat—margarine, butter, olive oil, or other oils. Finely diced cooked bacon or ham can be added with the fat and flour. Grated cheese sprinkled on just before serving is good. Finely sliced onion, garlic, shallots, or leeks add good flavor if stirred in before the final cooking; or sprinkle on a little powdered onion or garlic just before serving. After stirring in the flour, add ½ cup milk, cream, or undiluted evaporated milk and simmer 5 minutes, stirring often.

A few other members of this family also make good greens. Let's look at two or three.

Relatives of Good-King-Henry

Lamb's-Quarters *Chenopodium album*

This is a freely growing weed; the most delightful way to get rid of it is to eat it. When cooked like spinach, it is really good; if you want more flavor, add a handful of sour grass, *Rumex acetosella*. It can also be eaten raw. I've read that the seeds were gathered by the Indians and used for cereal or bread. I would hate to gather enough of the seeds for this, but I may try adding some to oatmeal or whole wheat bread.

Epazote *Chenopodium ambrosioides*

Epazote is considered a must in Mexican kitchens. It is used by many cooks there for seasoning certain beans and tamales. We know it as Mexican tea or wormseed. We probably would not cultivate it in our garden, but if found there, we might test it for seasoning a stew or a tea.

Orach *Atriplex hortensis*

Orach is known as mountain spinach. If you can secure it in the wild or at a grocery or a health store, you should find it very good as greens. It has been claimed to be the first plant known to have been cultivated for food. It was introduced into America in 1806, but I have not been able to find it in the market or listed in seed catalogues.

Beets, chard, and spinach are members of the goosefoot (Chenopodiaceae) family that we know best and are an essential part of many gardens. They are not classed as herbs, but I thought you would like to know that they are close relatives of Good-King-Henry.

Horehound   *Marrubium vulgare*

Horehound was used centuries ago for diseases of the throat and lungs. Many still find horehound candy soothing to the throat and horehound tea a comforting drink. Horehound is a bushy perennial (not always winter-hardy in very cold regions). It has lovely gray-green leaves crinkled at the edges. It is grown in home gardens for kitchen use but is also an interesting plant for the flower beds; pinch off the top if it is growing taller than you wish. If kept at a convenient size, it can add charm to the kitchen window-sill herb garden, where it will provide leaves for an occasional cup of tea. Like many of our herbs horehound belongs to the mint family, but unlike most of them it is practically odorless. However, back in 1600 it was included in a list of "herbs of good smell."

Although used medicinally and in beer and in candy for a long time, it is only fairly recently that its value in the kitchen has been recognized. It has a characteristic bitter taste that is now recommended in herb cook books for use as a seasoning for meat, stews, sauces, cakes, cookies, candy, and herb tea. It also is promising as a flavoring for the stronger-tasting vegetables. I tried it recently in hominy—it was good. I intend to try it with beans, squash, rutabagas, carrots, and kale, and I expect to like the results.

Horehound is one of the herbs where it is especially important to start with just a little until you have learned how much you will like. If you use only a leaf of fresh horehound or a pinch of the dried, you should find the food you are cooking unusually good—but if you use too much you may never want to try it again.

Hominy and Beef

1 tablespoon bacon fat or margarine
1 medium-sized onion, thinly sliced
½ cup celery, thinly sliced
1 pound ground beef
1 15-ounce can hominy

1 4-ounce can mushroom pieces and stems
1 teaspoon salt
¼ teaspoon dried horehound OR 1 leaf fresh horehound, finely cut

Melt fat in skillet; add onion and celery; stir and cook 2−3 minutes. Add beef; stir until well mixed (easiest to do with a fork, especially

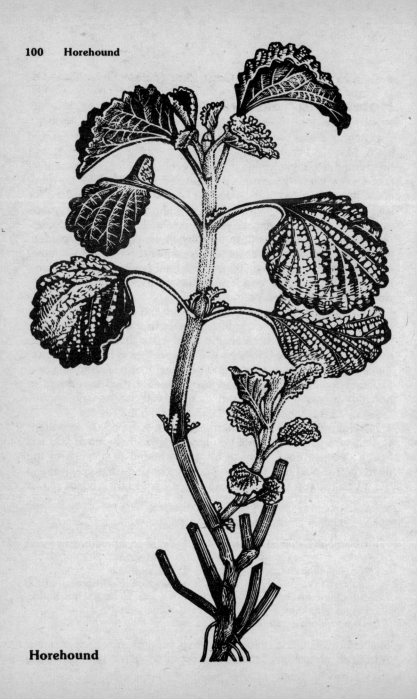

Horehound

an old-fashioned granny fork). Cook, stirring constantly, until meat is no longer red. Add hominy, mushrooms, and seasonings. Cover and cook over low heat, just barely boiling, for 10 minutes. Stir frequently and add water if needed to prevent sticking and burning.

Horehound Candy

2 cups horehound tea   1½ cups dark corn syrup
4 cups sugar   1 tablespoon butter or margarine

Pour horehound tea (*below*) into large kettle, so it will not boil over while cooking. Add sugar and syrup; stir until sugar is dissolved. Cook to hard-crack stage (300 F.) without stirring. Remove from stove; add butter and stir until blended. Pour into large well-buttered shallow pan, 15½ x 10½ x 1. When candy begins to harden, mark in squares; break apart when cold. Yields about 2½ pounds of candy. I wonder what mint candy would be like if it was made by this recipe, using strong mint tea instead of horehound tea.

Horehound Tea for Candy

½ cup fresh horehound leaves,   3 cups boiling water
    loosely packed

Cover and steep over low heat 15 minutes. Strain.

Horehound Tea to Drink

Use half as much, or less, of fresh leaves for 3 cups of water. A pinch of dried horehound leaves can be substituted. Steep as above. Good either hot or cold. When chilled it is an acceptable substitute for root beer. A leaf of horehound can be added when steeping a quart of regular or "store" tea.

See also Herb Honey.

Horseradish

Horseradish *Armoracia rusticana*

There is not any question about horseradish belonging to the mustard family. It has the characteristic sharp pungency, much more pronounced than its relatives, turnips and cabbage. It is an undemanding plant, winter-hardy and easy to grow almost anywhere. While it does not demand much care, it does like lots of room. It has many freely branching roots which are happy to spread in all directions. It is wise, they say, to dig it all up once a year and replant the small roots. The large roots can be prepared in various ways for use throughout the winter, or they may be dried to be used as needed.

Horseradish has been cultivated for over 1,000 years, first as medicine and later for seasoning. In the early 1800's plants were found in many of our pioneer gardens. They are again popular with many gardeners. Perhaps because of its high vitamin content—reported to be twice that of orange juice—it was thought to be necessary in household gardens. Its popularity is due not only to its vitamins and possible minerals but even more to the added flavor it gives our food.

Horseradish Leaves

Very young leaves can be eaten as a salad or added to tossed salads. A handful of young leaves cooked with some of the rather tasteless greens adds an appreciated zest. Try it with comfrey.

Horseradish Roots

The roots are the part most often used. They may be made into a sauce for meat, fish, or vegetables, or they may be mixed with butter or vinegar to be used as a seasoning. Horseradish relish and horseradish jelly add interest to meat and vegetable dishes. Some claim horseradish is absolutely essential in the cocktail sauce for oysters or other shellfish.

Whether you have dug roots from your garden or bought them from the market, the preparation will be the same. If they are rather dry you will find them easier to work with if you soak them in water for a few hours. Cut off the rootlets and scrape the roots. Some rootlets may be large enough to use; scrape them, too. Wash and dry the roots. Now they are ready to grate, grind, or run through the electric blender. My first experience with horseradish was grating it for my grandmother. I can still remember how my eyes smarted. A later experience in preparing it was putting it through the blender—I thought for a moment that I would hit the ceiling when I bent over the blender as I removed the top. I still use the blender but I don't lean over it when I remove the top. The horseradish is ready to use as soon as it is grated or ground. If not to be used soon, it can be put into a jar and white vinegar poured over to cover it.

Horseradish Butter

The simplest way to make horseradish butter is to add 1 or 2 tablespoons of well-drained prepared horseradish to ½ cup margarine or butter. Stir until well blended. Of course you can grate or grind the root and add it with a little lemon juice or vinegar to the margarine. With either method salt and pepper or paprika can be added. This butter gives piquancy when added to vegetables or spread on meat. Try it some time on buns for frankfurters. If you want just enough horseradish butter for a single serving, mix a teaspoon or less of horseradish with a tablespoon of margarine. It is easier to make this butter if the margarine or butter has been kept at room temperature for an hour or two.

Horseradish Vinegar

1 quart vinegar, white wine or distilled
¼ cup grated horseradish
1 tablespoon minced shallots or onion (optional)
½ teaspoon cayenne pepper (optional)

Bring vinegar just to boiling point. Add horseradish and seasonings if used. Pour into sterilized jars and shake well. Cover and keep in warm place 10 days, shaking well every day or two. Sample it; if you want a more pronounced flavor, let it stand a few more days. Strain if you want a clear vinegar; pour into sterilized bottles and seal.

This vinegar can be used to season salads or added to vegetables before serving. A tablespoonful can be added to the water in which fish is poached. Use plenty of imagination!

Horseradish Jelly

4½ cups sugar	½ cup grated horseradish
¾ cup vinegar	½ cup liquid pectin
¼ cup water	

In a large kettle stir sugar with vinegar and water; mix well. Add horseradish and stir until sugar is dissolved. Bring slowly to a boil stirring constantly. Stir in pectin and bring to a full rolling boil; continue boiling 1 minute. Remove from stove and pour into sterilized glasses. Cover with melted paraffin; when cooled, add another thin layer of paraffin, tipping the glass to seal the edges. Cover glasses with tops, foil, or plastic wrap. Good with any meat dish. I like it on bread or crackers.

Horseradish Cranberry Relish

2 cups raw cranberries	¼ cup ground horseradish
½ cup sugar	1 tablespoon lemon juice

Put all ingredients in blender and run at low speed until completely mixed and the cranberries are as fine as you wish. Remove from blender; put in jars; cover and store in refrigerator 2 days or longer before using. Instead of using a blender, berries can be put through a grinder or finely sliced. Serve with meat, fish, or poultry. Very good as an accompaniment to meat loaf or ham.

Sour Cream Sauce

The simplest way is just to stir grated horseradish gradually into sour cream, tasting to see when you have enough. Salt to taste, add a little sugar; you may also want to add paprika or minced chives, prepared mustard, or dill.

Cream Sauce

¼ cup light cream	1 teaspoon sugar
1 tablespoon grated horseradish	¼ teaspoon salt
1 tablespoon vinegar	¼ teaspoon pepper

Combine all ingredients; bring to a boil.

Cream Sauce with Egg

1 tablespoon minced onion	1 cup light cream
2 tablespoons margarine	¼ cup grated horseradish
2 egg yolks	Salt and pepper to taste

Sauté minced onion in margarine over medium heat until it just begins to brown. Beat egg yolks slightly and stir into cream. Add horseradish and then eggs and cream to onions, stirring until well blended; cook while stirring until thickened. Add seasonings and serve hot.

Whipped Cream Sauce

1 tablespoon grated horseradish	2 tablespoons cold water
¼ teaspoon salt	½ cup heavy cream, whipped

Add horseradish and salt to water and mix well. After whipping cream, stir in horseradish gently. Store in refrigerator 20 minutes or longer before serving.

Variations: Add 1 teaspoon of garlic salt as you whip the cream, omitting salt. Add 2 tablespoons tart jelly (currant is good) when mixing horseradish and cream. Add ½ cup sweetened apple sauce and 1 tablespoon lemon juice when combining horseradish and whipped cream.

Horseradish Sauce with Beef Stock

2 tablespoons margarine	¼ cup grated horseradish
2 tablespoons flour	1 teaspoon sugar
1 cup beef stock	½ teaspoon salt
½ cup vinegar	

Melt margarine, remove from heat, and stir in the flour. Slowly stir in beef stock and then vinegar. Add horseradish, sugar, and salt, stirring until well mixed. Return to stove and simmer 10 minutes, stirring frequently. Serve hot. This is my recipe.

Variations: I have read one which calls only for horseradish, beef stock, butter, and flour—no vinegar or other seasonings. Method of cooking as above. In another recipe a chopped onion is sautéed in butter before the flour is added; it also calls for a whole clove added with the horseradish and removed before serving.

Easiest Horseradish Sauces

Probably the easiest of all sauces to make and possibly the best is to add a spoonful or more of grated horseradish or of commercial (or your own) prepared horseradish, to vinegar, French dressing, mayonnaise, or other salad dressing.

A little of any of these horseradish seasonings will add zest to meat, fish, poultry, or vegetables. Results are good even when so little is used that you cannot taste the horseradish, you only know that the food has more character. Personally, I like to have enough to really taste. Then even a dismal day seems to perk up.

Horseradish does not need to be made into a vinegar, jelly, relish, or sauce in order to season food. Fresh grated horseradish can be used as you would other spices or herbs to pep up your cooking. Dried grated horseradish, soaked first in a little water, can be used instead of the fresh if the fresh is not available during the winter. Try a little (just a very little the first time—you can add more the next time if you wish) in meat loaf, scrambled eggs, beans, spinach, other vegetables. This may add a happy sparkle to the meal.

See also Comfrey Greens, Deviled Eggs (Chervil), Pickled Nasturtium Seeds.

Jerusalem Artichoke   *Helianthus tuberosus*

You may not find Jerusalem artichoke in your herb book; perhaps not in your cookbook; I found recipes in only four of the dozen or more in which I looked. If it is there, it may be listed as "girasole" or "earth apple"—other names for this perennial member of the Composite family. I grow it in my herb garden because I like to eat the crisp tubers like radishes or slice them into a tossed salad. Also I like their bright yellow flowers. Many of our herbs were brought from Europe to these shores by early settlers. Jerusalem artichoke, however, had been cultivated by the Indians long before a white man arrived in the United States. It became a welcome food for our western explorers. In 1616, it is said, it was introduced into Europe.

Jerusalem artichoke is apparently native to New York State and west from there to Minnesota, south to Georgia. It spreads easily by roots and by seeds and is now widespread throughout much of the country, mentioned alike in wild flower and in weed books. It is a perennial plant, growing in a season to a height of 6 to 12 feet, dying down late in the fall and coming up again the next spring. In the garden it is decidedly a background plant! Late in the season after many plants are through blooming, it has tall many-flowered clusters of yellow sunflowerlike blossoms. The tubers when mature weigh 3 or 4 ounces, not quite as large as a potato. They are a good potato substitute for dieters, as they are low in starch. The white flesh has a crisp nutlike texture and a faintly sweet taste.

If used raw, the tubers should be scrubbed and peeled. After peeling keep them in cold water until used, as they turn dark if exposed to the air. If cooked, scrub them and cook for a few minutes before peeling. The skin can then be rubbed or peeled off. Here are suggestions for using them raw along with a few recipes for cooked artichokes.

Raw Jerusalem Artichokes

Scrub tubers, peel and slice them. I like them just as they are, but you may wish to season them, perhaps with onion or garlic salt.

For a crisp relish cover the slices with vinegar. Cover container and let stand in refrigerator a few hours or overnight.

Pickled Artichokes

For pickled artichokes boil for a few minutes, peel and quarter. Put into a jar and cover with vinegar. You may want to add a couple garlic cloves or an inch or two of horseradish root. Cover the jar and let stand a couple weeks.

Jerusalem Artichoke Salad

Because they are so delightfully crisp, I like them peeled, then sliced or diced and added to a tossed salad. If the tubers are the main ingredients of a salad, endive and/or leeks are a fine addition.

Cooked Jerusalem Artichoke

The cooked tubers can be substituted for potatoes in any potato salad recipe. Be sure not to cook them too long or they will be mushy.

After they are cooked and peeled, the tubers can be mashed, seasoned with salt, pepper, and margarine, reheated and served as potatoes. Or they can be diced, seasoned, and heated in a cream sauce.

Jerusalem Artichokes with Tomatoes

2 tablespoons tomato paste
¼ cup water
2 cups artichokes, cooked, peeled, and sliced
½ teaspoon dried basil OR 1 tablespoon fresh basil, minced
Salt and pepper to taste
2 tablespoons margarine

Mix tomato paste and water; add to artichokes and mix well. Pour into greased casserole, add seasonings, and dot with margarine. Bake at 375 F. until hot and bubbly, about 20—30 minutes. Tomato sauce, or seasoned cooked tomatoes can be substituted for the tomato paste. How much salt and pepper to add depends upon whether artichokes and tomatoes are already seasoned.

Jerusalem Artichoke with Cheese

2 tablespoons margarine
2 tablespoons flour
1 cup milk
2 cups artichokes, cooked, peeled, and sliced
Salt and pepper to taste
½ cup bread crumbs
¼ cup grated cheese

Make a cream sauce of the margarine, flour, and milk; add artichokes and seasonings. Put in greased casserole; sprinkle with bread crumbs and then with cheese. Bake at 375 F. until heated through and nicely browned, about 30 minutes.

Jerusalem Artichoke and Wieners

2 cups artichokes, cooked, peeled, and sliced	1 8-ounce can tomato sauce
4 wieners, sliced	1½ cups crushed corn flakes

After washing, boiling, peeling, and slicing artichokes, add sliced wieners, and mix with tomato sauce. Pour into casserole and cover with crushed corn flakes. Bake at 375 F. until bubbly and lightly browned, about 30 minutes.

Lavender *Lavandula angustifolia*
subsp. *angustifolia*

Back in the 1600's, Thomas Culpeper wrote, "Lavender is so well known, being an inhabitant of almost every garden, that it needeth no description." Earlier than that it was considered in Greece and Rome as almost an essential for perfuming the baths of the wealthy. Even today we might find a cup of lavender tea added to the bath water refreshing. Its name comes from the Latin word *lavare* meaning to wash. Today, centuries later, lavender (also called English lavender) is in much demand for soap, toilet water, and perfume. In smelling salts it is used to relieve faintness. Lavender tea is supposed to have a tonic effect. In the clothes closet it is one of the pleasantest of moth discouragers.

Lavender, like many other fragrant herbs, is a member of the mint family. It is a perennial well adapted to the flower bed because of its pleasing shape, its yearlong foliage, and its fragrance. I found few lavender recipes, but some authors mentioned the delicate flowery flavor of lavender honey, which is available in a few stores; others mentioned the added aromatic flavor of salads where lavender vinegar had been used in the dressing, or recommended the use of lavender in herb mixtures because of its pungent lemony or minty flavor. Long ago it was used to flavor salads, fruit desserts, jellies, drinks, and confections. With these suggestions and with imagination I have come up with the following recipes. If you enjoy their fragrant flavor, you may think of other ways to use lavender in your cooking. I use about twice as much of the lavender, either fresh or dried, as I have stated in these recipes. As with all recipes, it is well to start with only a little until you learn how much you like.

Lavender Tea

1 tablespoon lavender   1 pint cold water

Bring to a boil and simmer 10 minutes. Strain and serve either hot or cold.

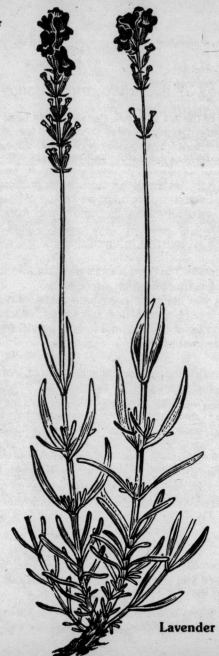

Lavender

Lavender Gelatin

2 cups lavender tea
1 3-ounce package lime or
   lemon gelatin

Bring 1 cup of the tea to a boil. Remove from heat; add gelatin and stir until dissolved; add the other cup of cold tea; stir. Chill until set; serve on chervil or lettuce leaves as a salad. With a ham sandwich and a hot drink it makes an excellent lunch.

Lavender Salad

4 dates, sliced
4 pecans, sliced
1 cup creamed cottage cheese
1 cup lavender gelatin, softened or diced

Pit and slice dates; shell and slice pecans. Put into bowl with cottage cheese and gelatin; mix lightly with a fork.

Variations: Raisins may be used instead of dates; other nuts substituted for pecans. Diced apples, bananas, or other fruit may be added. I consider the cottage cheese a salad dressing, but you may want to add mayonnaise.

Lavender Dessert

1 package chocolate-flavored
   pudding mix (3 ounces)
1 cup dried milk
½ cup crunchy peanut butter
1 teaspoon lavender leaves
2 cups warm water
1 cup tiny marshmallows or large
   ones, quartered

Mix pudding and dried milk; add peanut butter and lavender; stir until smooth. Gradually stir in the water and bring to a boil, stirring all the time. Add marshmallows and stir until blended and melted. Pour into serving dishes. Delicious warm or chilled.

Lavender Cookies

2 eggs
½ cup margarine
1 cup sugar
1 teaspoon lavender leaves
1½ cups flour
2 teaspoons baking powder
½ teaspoon salt

Put eggs, margarine, sugar, and lavender, in this order, into blender and run on low until well mixed. Sift flour, baking powder, and salt into a mixing bowl; add other ingredients and stir until well blended. Drop, a teaspoonful at a time, onto an ungreased cookie sheet. Bake at 375 F. until lightly browned, about 10 minutes.

Lavender Jelly

There are at least three ways to make lavender jelly. Use lavender tea for the liquid in a recipe for pectin jelly. Make a lavender-apple jelly by adding 1 teaspoon lavender to 1 quart apple juice and simmer for 10 minutes; strain and proceed as you would for apple jelly. (This might also be good with currant or grape jelly.) Or place lavender flowers and/or leaves in jelly glasses before pouring in plain apple jelly.

Lavender Conserve

A recipe for this, which I have not tested, is dated 1655, when it was printed in a cookbook by the cook to Queen Henrietta Maria of England. Lavender flowers were beaten with three times their weight of sugar until completely blended.

See also Lemon Verbena; Chocolate Cookies (Lemon Verbena); *and* Herb Honey, Herb Vinegar.

Leek

Leek *Allium ampeloprasum* Porrum Group

Leeks, prized for centuries in Europe, are becoming more appreciated in America. Although they have a strong odor, fortunately lost in cooking, they are one of the sweetest, mildest-tasting members of the onion family. Dioscorides, a physician when Nero was Emperor of Rome, recommended leeks for the throat; it has been said that Nero ate only leeks and oil on certain days of the month to keep his singing voice in trim. The Welsh pay tribute to the leek as the Irish do the shamrock. It is supposed to be a symbol of strength; each Welsh soldier wore leeks in his cap during a winning fight with the Saxons. Perhaps their belief in its magic did give them more stamina in their fighting. And maybe its vitamins and minerals can give us more strength for joyous living. To this day many a Welshman proudly wears a fresh leek in his buttonhole on March first.

Leeks can be used raw or cooked, fresh or frozen, as a vegetable or as seasoning. Finely cut tender young leaves can be substituted for chives as a garnish on mashed potatoes, cottage cheese, tossed or gelatin salads.

The tenderer inner leaves of leeks can be substituted in any recipe calling for green onions or scallions, the bulbs in recipes calling for onions or shallots. Leeks are known in France as "the poor man's asparagus" and can be cooked as you would cook asparagus. Added to a white sauce and poured over toast, they are better than asparagus. Leeks are a fine addition to soups, salads, vegetables, and meat dishes. The question has been asked "What is lamb stew without leeks?" Others ask the same about potato soup.

Potato and Leek Soup

⅔ cup leeks
1 tablespoon margarine
1 cup diced potatoes
    (1 medium-sized potato)

2 cups boiling water
½ teaspoon salt
⅔ cup powdered milk

Wash leeks carefully and cut into thin slices, using all except the tough outer leaves. Melt margarine, add leeks and cook a few minutes. Add potatoes, boiling water, and salt. Cook until vegetables are soft, about 15 minutes. Slowly stir in the powdered milk, and serve hot.

Variations: Each serving can be topped with finely cut chives, chervil, or parsley. If you have a little more or less than a cupful of potatoes, adjust the other ingredients a little. Leeks are good also in other soups—try them in bean, pea, or mushroom soup.

Leeks and Cheese

6 slices bread	½ can water
1 tablespoon margarine	½ teaspoon salt
1 cup chopped leeks	⅛ teaspoon dried powdered
3 eggs	thyme
1 can condensed cream of	1 cup grated cheese
mushroom soup	

Toast bread and cut into small cubes; melt the margarine and wilt leeks in it; beat eggs and add to soup, water, salt, and thyme; mix well. Mix bread and leeks and put half in a greased casserole, next add half the egg mixture, and top with half of cheese. Repeat. Bake at 350 F. until an inserted knife comes out clean, 45–60 minutes.

Variations: Try this recipe with cooked noodles or spaghetti instead of toast. Try it with onions instead of leeks.

Leeks for Lunch

2 cups leeks	4 slices bread
½ teaspoon salt	Butter or margarine
1 cup boiling water	Cheese (optional)
2 cups white sauce	Parsley (optional)
4 eggs	

Remove old dried outer leaves; wash leeks carefully; cut into inch-long pieces (both tops and bulbs); cook until tender in salted water, about 10 minutes; stir into white sauce. Poach eggs; toast and butter bread (I use margarine). Put toast on individual serving plates; pour on white sauce and top with eggs. Sprinkle with grated cheese, or garnish with parsley if you wish; but I like it very much just as it is.

Lamb Stew

3 pounds lamb neck	½ cup carrots, in 1-inch pieces
3 tablespoons flour	½ cup snap beans, in 1-inch pieces
2 tablespoons vegetable oil	pieces
1 cup water	½ cup celery, in 1-inch pieces
1 teaspoon salt	1 cup potatoes, in fairly large
1 cup leeks in 1-inch pieces	cubes

Coat meat with flour, brown in heated oil (I use a heavy iron Dutch oven), add a cup of water, and cook 2 hours, stirring occasionally. (I do this a day, or at least several hours, before I want the stew.) When it has cooled, place in refrigerator for fat to harden, so as to be removed. An hour before serving time, take meat from refrigerator, remove hardened fat, bring to a boil, add salt and vegetables. Cover and cook until vegetables are done 30−40 minutes.

Variations: Sometimes I use boneless lamb shoulder or breast (2 pounds are enough), cubing meat before browning it, but there is more flavor in stews made from neck pieces. Other vegetables can be substituted or added: peas, corn, and tomatoes are good. Herbs can be added: any of the culinary ones, especially basil, cumin, marjoram, fenugreek, or rosemary. Potatoes can be omitted, and spaghetti, noodles, or rice added. Or the stew can be topped with dumplings (*below*).

Dumplings for Stew

1 egg	1 cup flour
½ cup milk	2 teaspoons baking powder
2 tablespoons vegetable oil	½ teaspoon salt

Beat egg and milk together until blended. Add oil and sift in remaining ingredients, stirring lightly until blended. Drop by spoonfuls onto hot stew. Cook 7 minutes covered and 7 more uncovered. If dumplings are large, cook a minute or two longer.

Leeks, Lentils, and Sausage

½ pound link sausage	1 cup canned tomatoes
2½ cups cooked lentils	1 cup sliced cooked leeks

Cut sausages in quarters or smaller and brown. Mix with other ingredients. Pour into a 2-quart casserole and bake at 350 F. for 30 minutes.

Coleslaw

2½ cups cabbage   ¼ cup vinegar
 ½ cup leeks   1 teaspoon salt
 ½ cup cream

Grate or chop cabbage; peel and slice leeks. Slowly add vinegar
to cream, stirring steadily. Combine ingredients. Season with salt.
  Variations: Add pepper, sugar, and herbs if you wish. We have
always used the cream and vinegar dressing, but this salad is also
good with a cooked salad dressing or any of your preferred commercial dressings.

Fruit Salad with Leeks

1 apple   2 tablespoons cottage cheese
1 orange   1 tablespoon mayonnaise
¼ cup sliced leeks   1 tablespoon nut meats
2 dates

Wash, peel, and slice apple and orange. Carefully wash and slice
leeks. Remove seeds from dates and slice them. Mix cottage cheese
and mayonnaise and toss all ingredients together. Here are carbohydrates and proteins, fruit, calories, minerals, and vitamins for a
complete meal, especially if eaten with celery or carrot sticks, a slice
of bread and a glass of milk.

  See also Egg Sandwich Filling (Shallots), Fish with Sorrel, Jerusalem Artichoke Salad, Parsley Butter, Potato Salad (Sorrel), Sesame Creamed Chicken, Shallot Soup, Sorrel Soup; *and* Herb
Butter.

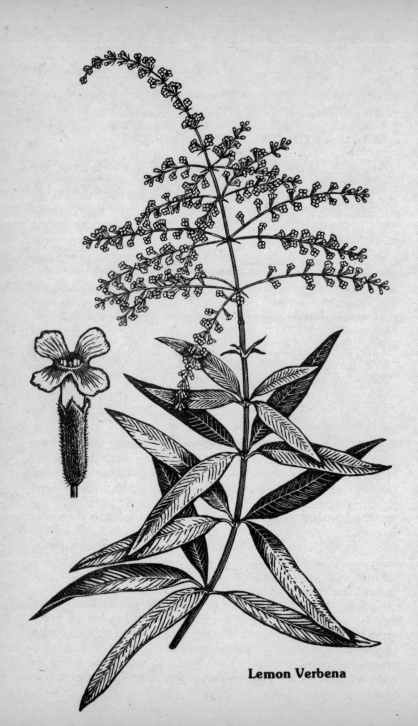

Lemon Verbena

Lemon Verbena *Aloysia triphylla*

This herb was well loved by our forefathers (or I should say our forebears), but they did not bring it from Europe. Lemon verbena is native to South America. It is reported to have been taken to Europe in 1784 and to have been readily accepted there as a culinary herb and also as a medicinal one. About the same time a New England sea captain is said to have brought it home from Chile. Lemons at that time were not a New England staple, and lemon verbena was gladly used to flavor fruits and other desserts. It was also a good substitute for the tea that patriots were no longer drinking.

The long slim leaves are exceptionally fragrant. When barely touched they give off a warm aroma called "the most ravishing lemon odor known to man." They have a lemony flavor as well as a lemony fragrance. They can be used wherever a mild lemon taste is wanted, are good with lemon juice or alone in cooking, and make a fine tea alone or added to Oriental tea.

The surest way to have lemon verbena leaves for cooking is to buy a plant from an herb dealer or to start a cutting from a friend who has a plant. In the south they are winter-hardy. In the north they can be a year-round house plant or can be moved outdoors for the summer. Lemon verbenas lose most of their leaves when brought in, but new ones will grow—I threw away a plant once before I learned that this would happen. Gather up the leaves and dry them for cooking or for fragrance bags; better yet pick off the leaves when you bring the plant indoors. With proper care—a sunny window and a weekly shower bath—lemon verbenas will live a long time as house plants. When your daughter marries, she may want your plant as an heirloom! I have heard of them being passed on from one generation to the next. Cuttings root easily, and I like to have small plants on hand to give to friends.

You may enjoy the fragrance so much that you will hate to harvest the leaves for cooking. But lemon verbenas in a few years will grow tall and straggly if not pruned; when pruned they are most decorative. The prunings are delightful in the fireplace and in fragrance jars or bags; even more delightful in any recipe calling for mint, lavender, or the fragrant-leaved geraniums; best of all in tea.

Lemon Verbena in Salads

Lemon verbena leaves placed at bottom of salad plates add a fragrant touch to fruit salads. Use lemon verbena tea (see Herb Tea) in making gelatin base for salads. Shredded leaves make an attractive garnish for salads.

Lemon Verbena Fruit Cup

Cut leaves fine and stir into fruit or keep leaves whole and place in bottom of cup or on top of fruit.

Lemon Verbena Puddings

Add 2 or 3 finely cut lemon verbena leaves to bread pudding, rice, gelatin, cornstarch puddings, or custards; use more leaves if less than 2 inches long.

Herb Custard

1 egg
1 tablespoon sugar
Pinch salt

⅔ cup milk
2 lemon verbena leaves, minced

In top of double boiler beat egg, sugar, salt, milk, and finely minced lemon verbena leaves. Cook over boiling water about 15 minutes or until custard coats the spoon. Pour into serving dish. Serve either warm or cold, but standing a few hours in the refrigerator improves the flavor. This custard can easily serve as dessert for two, but it is not too sweet or rich to be the main part of lunch or supper for one person if served with fruit, cheese, crackers, and a hot drink.

Variations: Use more verbena leaves, but better less the first time. Leaves of rosemary, pineapple sage, or any of the fragrant-leaved geraniums can be used instead of lemon verbena. Sliced fresh strawberries or peaches, sugared lightly, are fine to serve on top.

Lemon Verbena Cake

Substitute lemon verbena leaves for geranium leaves in Mrs. Kenerson's Sponge Cake. Or put leaves in bottom of cake pan for any cake recipe.

Lemon Verbena Cookies

Make dainty cookies by placing a sugar cookie on top of lemon verbena leaves. Finely cut leaves can be added to any cookie recipe, omitting other flavoring. I used the blender for the chocolate cookies (*below*), but they can be made following the method for sugar cookies and using finely cut leaves instead of blending them.

Chocolate Cookies

1½ cups flour	½ cup brown sugar
2 teaspoons baking powder	¼ cup cocoa
½ teaspoon salt	2 eggs
½ cup margarine	2 teaspoons lemon verbena
½ cup white sugar	¼ cup milk

Sift flour, baking powder, and salt into mixing bowl. Put remaining ingredients into blender and run on low until completely mixed, about a minute or two. Pour into flour and stir until completely mixed. Drop teaspoonfuls on ungreased cookie sheet and bake at 375 F. 8–10 minutes.

Variations: Also delicious when made with anise, caraway, lavender, or mint.

Lemon Verbena Jelly

Follow directions for Lavender Jelly using lemon verbena leaves. Or for just a slight additional flavor, put a few leaves in bottom of jelly glasses before pouring in jelly—especially good with apple jelly.

See also Sugarless Cookies (Cardamom); *and* Herb Butter, Herb Tea.

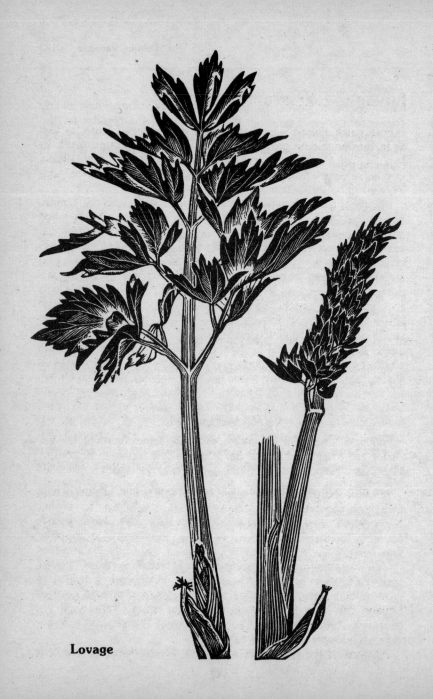

Lovage

Lovage   *Levisticum officinale*

Fortunately lovage is gaining in favor in the United States as well as in Europe. Some grow it as a handsome background plant. Its large, glossy, fernlike leaves, its tall stalks with their umbrellalike umbels of yellow flowers give it a striking tropical appearance, adding distinction to the flower bed.

Lovage is a member of the Parsley family along with dill, coriander, fennel, and a number of other herbs. It has also been called sea parsley and love parsley. The last name may be most appropriate; a friend quoted her children as saying "It's called lovage because we love it." It is one of the oldest known salad plants, with records extending far back. It was grown in a Swiss monastery garden in the 9th century. It has been cultivated in England for at least six centuries. It was brought from there by our early settlers and was a favorite in colonial gardens. They liked it because it was an easily cultivated, long-lived perennial which served them in many ways. It was ornamental in their gardens. It gave them fragrance which they used in their linen closets, perhaps in their bath water. It is said that they dried the roots and took fragrant pieces to church with them, chewing while listening to long and perhaps often boring sermons. I wonder if it would help solve the obesity problem in the United States if we chewed lovage while watching TV! Surely the colonists raised it for its medicinal qualities—it had long been grown in Europe as a remedy for eye, throat, and other troubles. But probably the principal reason for growing lovage was as seasoning in food.

It has a sharp but rather warm celery flavor that adds much to meat and vegetables. It has been used as a substitute for celery, pepper, and caraway. I'm sure they were glad to be able to raise a flavoring for their food instead of buying the expensive imported seasonings.

You may have trouble finding lovage, fresh or dried, leaves, seeds or roots in grocery or health stores. Fortunately it is easy to grow with ordinary care in the flower, vegetable, or herb garden. Lovage can also be an attractive house plant. Trim back occasionally so that it does not become too tall. This pruning will provide fresh leaves and leaves to dry.

All parts of the plant offer seasoning. Fresh, dried, or frozen, it

can be used anywhere that you want the flavor of celery. I use it
often in soups and stews. Just rubbing the salad bowl with a lovage
leaf gives celery taste to the salad; you may like to use it even if you
have celery in the salad. Cooked leaves have been recommended
as a substitute for spinach, but I think it better to use them with
other greens—they are a very good addition to comfrey. Fresh leaflets are a fine garnish for fish or for a vegetable casserole. Try adding a leaf to beans, potatoes, or other vegetables a few minutes
before they finish cooking. Lovage stalks have been candied. Lovage wine was once popular. Lovage seeds are good in salad dressings; also instead of caraway seeds in corn bread or rye bread. The
leaves, fresh or dried, make an especially delightful tea—fragrant,
restful, and relaxing.

Edible-Pod Peas

2 cups edible-pod peas	1 tablespoon margarine or
½ teaspoon salt	bacon fat
1 tablespoon fresh lovage OR 1 teaspoon dried lovage	½ cup boiling water

Wash peas, remove ends, cut or snap into 1-inch pieces (or leave
whole if you wish). Add with salt and lovage to the boiling water
and cook about 15 minutes until tender but not too soft—some like
them crisper. Drain, add margarine or other fat—bacon fat is
good—and serve.
Variations: Good, also, served with a white sauce or with grated
cheese.

Tuna Fish Sandwiches

1 cup flaked tuna fish	Mayonnaise to moisten
2 tablespoons minced lovage leaves OR 2 teaspoons crumbled dried lovage leaves	

Combine all ingredients and spread on buttered bread.

Lovage in Salads

Fresh or dried lovage leaves or lovage seeds can be added to almost any salad; they are especially good in coleslaw or in fish salads. I was surprised when I read that cooked lovage roots were used as a salad in some European countries. They cook and slice the roots; add oil, vinegar, and salt to them. I'm not sure that I would like that salad, but I recommend this one.

1½ cups diced cooked potatoes	¼ cup mayonnaise
¾ cup cooked and diced lovage roots	Salt
	Paprika

Prepare potatoes and lovage roots. Add mayonnaise and salt to taste; if potatoes and lovage were salted as they cooked, you may not need more salt. Spoon into salad bowl and sprinkle with paprika.

Other Uses for Lovage

Substitute for celery.

See also A Corn Bread Dinner (Cumin), Sage and Cottage Cheese Bread; *and* Greens, Herb Tea.

Marjoram

Marjoram   *Origanum majorana*

This is the sweet or knotted marjoram, not the pot or the wild marjoram, although they can be used in the same way; sweet marjoram, often simply called marjoram, has a somewhat better taste, but all are fine in cooking. This is also known as *amaraco* and as *Wurstkraut* (sausage vegetable). I like best the name "Joy of the Mountain," which is often applied to it in its native Mediterranean home. It is a delightfully fragrant member of the mint family, said to be one of the most pleasantly scented of all herbs. It has for many centuries been one of the best-loved herbs.

Sweet marjoram was once found in almost every kitchen garden. It is now becoming increasingly popular because of its fragrance in the garden and its aromatic taste in the kitchen. It was brought to America from England by the early settlers; they wanted it in their tea. It is an attractive plant in the garden and in the house. With its foot-high, freely branching stems it looks like a sturdy little shrub. It has downy light-green leaves and very small clustered creamy white flowers; its flower heads look like tiny knobs or knots. Sweet marjoram, a tender perennial, not winter-hardy in the north, is usually grown as an annual. But if a plant is potted, kept indoors during freezing weather, then replanted outdoors, it sometimes lives for many years, giving freely of fragrance and flavor. Or it may be planted in a pot as a permanent house plant. The leaves are the part most frequently used, although all of the plant is fragrant. Leaves are best gathered just as the plants begin to bloom, but there is plenty of seasoning power in the tiny seedlings pulled up when one is thinning the crop. It keeps its seasoning ability when dried or frozen. Dried marjoram can be readily purchased at many grocery stores and plants from greenhouses which feature herbs.

Sweet marjoram is an obliging herb, adding its spicy flavor to many foods; perhaps not to desserts, but that may be just because no one has used it in desserts. It has been called the kitchen magician, also the herb with a thousand uses. It adds a spicy flavor to eggs, cheese, meat, fish, poultry, to almost any vegetable. It is good in soups, stews, salads, in hot or cold drinks. Just add a little marjoram to your recipes for the above foods and see if you do not agree that it truly has magic in the kitchen. Incidentally, if you are ever "down in the dumps," brew yourself a cup of marjoram tea;

the herbalist John Gerard in 1597 wrote, "Sweet marjoram is good for those who are given to overmuch sighing." It still is; also it is enjoyed by those of a cheerful disposition! Here are some recipes I have adapted for my use of marjoram. They are also good with other culinary herbs.

Marjoram Biscuits

2 cups flour
4 teaspoons baking powder
1 teaspoon salt
2 teaspoons dried marjoram
    leaves

¼ cup shortening
¾ cup milk

Combine dry ingredients. Cut in fat rather coarsely. Make a hole in the middle and add milk. Stir only until combined. Put out on lightly floured board and knead as for bread approximately 12 times. Roll out to 1-inch thickness, cut and bake at 450 F. about 15 minutes.

Toast and Egg

This is the first recipe of mine that was ever printed. It appeared in 1908 in a Grange cookbook as a contribution from the Juvenile Grange of Delta, Washington. Its name was "Baked Toast." "Prepare toast in the ordinary way, and as each slice is ready, dip quickly into a pan of boiling water, slightly salted; then put in a baking dish, sprinkle well with salt, and cover deep with boiling milk; bake in a dish, closely covered, for 15 minutes. Heat 3 or 4 tablespoons of cream before sending to the table." I varied it in the following way for a hearty breakfast. It is equally good for lunch or supper. Other herbs could be used, fresh instead of reconstituted dried milk, margarine instead of cream (as a child I lived on a farm where cream and fresh milk were available); I added an egg and baked it longer just because I like my egg well cooked.

⅓ cup powdered milk
¾ cup warm water
⅛ teaspoon salt
1 tablespoon margarine

¼ teaspoon crumbled dried
    marjoram
1 slice toast
1 egg

Dissolve milk in water; add salt, margarine, and marjoram. Bring to a boil; pour over toast in small casserole. Break egg on top of toast; bake 20 minutes at 350 F.

Veal Cutlets

1 teaspoon salt
1 teaspoon crumbled dried
   marjoram OR 1 tablespoon
   minced fresh marjoram
1 cup bread crumbs, finely
   crumbled

4 veal cutlets
1 egg, beaten with
1 tablespoon water
⅓ cup cooking oil

Stir salt and marjoram into bread crumbs. Dip cutlets in egg beaten with water and then in seasoned crumbs. Pour oil into 10-inch skillet and heat. Over moderate flame, cook cutlets in the oil 15 minutes; turn and cook 15 minutes on other side. If available, garnish with sprigs of fresh marjoram.

Sweet Potato Casserole

2 cups sliced sweet potatoes
1 medium onion, finely sliced
1 cup canned peas
¼ cup liquid from peas

½ teaspoon crumbled dried
   marjoram
1 tablespoon margarine

Combine all ingredients and mix well. Bake at 350 F. until vegetables are tender, about 40 minutes.

Turnips with Marjoram

3 cups diced turnips
1 tablespoon margarine or other
   shortening

1 cup water
1 teaspoon dried marjoram
½ teaspoon salt

Put all ingredients into a kettle. Cover and cook about 15 minutes until turnips are tender—time depends on age and size of turnips. Add more water if needed to prevent burning.
Variations: The same recipe can be used for carrots and other vegetables.

Apple Salad

2 cups diced apples
¼ cup seeded raisins
½ cup canned mandarin oranges
½ teaspoon dried marjoram

2 tablespoons mayonnaise
   diluted with
1 tablespoon mandarin orange
   juice

Toss apples, raisins, and mandarin oranges together lightly. Mix marjoram, mayonnaise, and orange juice. Add to fruit and toss lightly.

Variations: Dates could be used instead of raisins. Bananas, nut meats, and/or marshmallows can be added.

See also Deviled Eggs (Chervil), Herb Bread (Savory), Lamb Stew (Leek), Macaroni for Salad (Comfrey), Potato Salad (Sorrel), Pot Roast with Thyme, Scrambled Eggs (Basil), Thyme in an Oven Roast, Tomato Omelet with Herbs (Sage), Zucchini Squash Casserole (Basil); *and* Herb Honey, Herb Jelly, Herb Vinegar.

Apple Mint

Mint *Mentha*

There are many different mints known to scientists. Of these I grow four to use in my kitchen—apple mint, lemon mint (also known as orange or bergamot mint), peppermint, and spearmint. I enjoy them in the garden for their vigorous growth and their attractive leaves, and especially for their fragrance as I touch them in passing. I like to have one as a house plant; at present I have a lemon mint on the kitchen window sill—I can have a fragrant cup of mint tea whenever I wish. In summer I like a bouquet of mint on the dining room table. The purplish flowers are a quiet foil for brilliant nasturtiums and calendulas. I pinch the leaves just before dinnertime for fragrance.

In medieval days mints were among the best-loved strewing herbs for cathedral floors. Banquet tables were rubbed with mint to release the fragrance, to protect from pestilence, and to stimulate appetites. Mint strewn on city streets added a welcoming touch to triumphal entries; rubbed on teeth it gave a sweet-smelling mouth. Mint served as money when the Hebrews used it as a tithing herb. It was grown in monastery gardens as a medicinal herb—Thomas Culpeper in the 17th century mentioned about forty ailments for which mint was prescribed. To smell mint cleared the head; taken as a tea it was soothing to the stomach and good for the memory; added to the bath water it calmed nerves and strengthened muscles; or so many believed in the long ago.

Mint was one of the "precious herbs" brought by the Pilgrim Fathers to New England. It was grown in many gardens, probably for some of these benefits, possibly for mint juleps, surely for seasoning food. I like the old New England custom of giving a mint root to a guest. The earliest culinary reference to mint may have been in the 3rd century when a writer referred to mint sauce. Think how many generations since then have known the tantalizing flavor of mint sauce!

Here are two recipes for sauce. Either is good with lamb or mutton. Try them, too, with meat loaf, hamburgers, frankfurters, and with vegetables such as winter squash, sweet potatoes, and baked beans.

Mint Sauce

¼ cup sugar
¼ teaspoon salt
¼ cup water

½ cup vinegar
¼ cup finely cut mint

Stir sugar and salt into water; add vinegar; bring to a boil and simmer uncovered 5 minutes. Pour over mint and let stand 30 minutes. Strain out leaves or not, as you wish. Serve hot or cold.

Honey Mint Sauce

Substitute ¾ cup strained honey for the sugar and follow directions for Mint Sauce.

Oatmeal Porridge

This is the way I cooked cereal during the years that my husband was on a salt-free diet. Now I add salt, a scant ½ teaspoon, and I still like it with mint. If the mint is fresh I use 1 tablespoon of finely minced leaves. The proportion of oatmeal and water and the length of cooking depends upon whether the regular or quick cooking oatmeal is used; the amount depends upon how well you like porridge. This recipe is for 2 servings; I keep half of it in the refrigerator and warm it up or fry it for a second day.

⅔ cup oats
½ teaspoon salt (omit for a salt-
    free diet)
1½ cups water

1 teaspoon crumbled dried mint
    OR 1 tablespoon finely
    minced fresh leaves

Add oats, salt, and mint to briskly boiling water. Stir well and cook on low heat for 5–10 minutes. Remove from heat, stir again, cover, let stand 5 minutes. Serve with cream, apple sauce, or butter and brown sugar.

Minted Carrots

2 cups carrots, peeled and sliced
½ teaspoon salt
½ scant teaspoon crumbled dried
    mint OR 1 teaspoon fresh
    mint, minced

¾ cup boiling water
1 tablespoon margarine
    (optional)

Add carrots, salt, and mint to boiling water; cook until carrots are tender, 15–20 minutes for new carrots, or as long as 40 minutes for old ones. Add more water if needed to prevent burning. Add margarine before serving if desired. P.S.: This recipe was written and printed some time ago. I no longer cook the carrots until soft; I now like them somewhat crisp.

Mint Vinegar

Mint vinegar can be made by the standard Herb Vinegar recipe, or you may prefer this sweetened version.

2 cups minced and crushed mint leaves	1 quart vinegar
	1 cup sugar

Add sugar and mint to cold vinegar. Stir while bringing it slowly to a boil; simmer 5 minutes. Strain; pour into sterilized bottles; cork tightly. Use in making sauces or salad dressings.

Lemon Mint

Devil's Food Cake

4 squares unsweetened chocolate	1 egg
½ cup sugar	¼ cup sour milk
½ cup sweet milk	1⅛ cups flour
1 egg yolk	½ teaspoon soda
¼ cup butter	½ teaspoon commercial peppermint extract
½ cup sugar	

Melt chocolate over hot water, add ½ cup sugar, and gradually sweet milk; then add egg yolk, and cook until mixture thickens. Set aside to cool. Cream butter, add gradually ½ cup sugar, egg well beaten, sour milk, and flour mixed and sifted with soda. Combine mixtures and add peppermint. Bake in 2 round 8-inch pans 20–25 minutes at 350 F. Put boiled frosting between layers and on top. Add to frosting between layers ¼ cup seeded raisins cut in pieces, if desired.

Baked Apples

6 baking apples	1 teaspoon dried mint, crumbled
¼ cup brown sugar	6 tablespoons water
¼ cup raisins	

Wash and core apples; place in casserole or deep pie plate. Combine sugar, raisins, and mint; fill apple cavities; and add water. Bake at 350 F. 45 minutes to 1 hour, until done. The time depends on the variety of apples.

Chocolate Sundae Sauce

2 squares unsweetened chocolate	⅛ teaspoon salt
1 tablespoon cornstarch	¼ cup corn syrup
½ cup sugar	½ cup mint tea (see Herb Tea)

Grate chocolate or cut into small pieces. Mix cornstarch, sugar, and salt; add corn syrup and stir until well blended. Add chocolate to mint tea and bring slowly to a boil. Add other ingredients and cook, stirring constantly until sauce begins to thicken. Serve hot or chilled over ice cream.

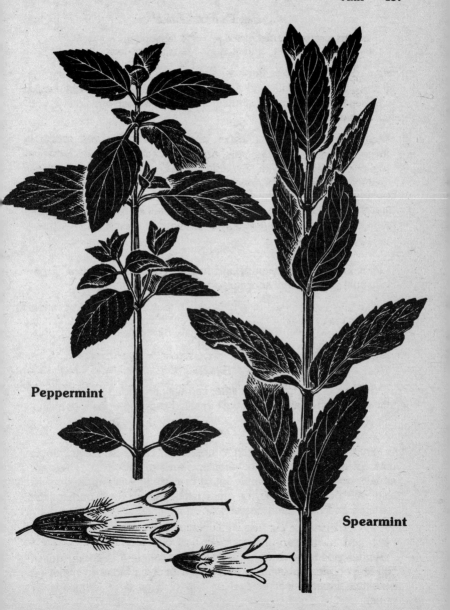

Peppermint

Spearmint

A Quick Cup of Chocolate

2 tablespoons chocolate chips   2 tablespoons hot water
¼ teaspoon dried mint, crumbled   ¾ cup milk

Stir chocolate and mint into water and bring slowly to a boil, stirring all the time. Add milk and again bring to a boil, still stirring. Add whipped cream or a substitute topping or a marshmallow if you wish; I like it just as it is.

Other Uses for Mint in Cooking

There are many more ways in which mint adds a happy flavor to cooking. I hope these will suggest to you still more uses of the fragrant, flavorful mints. Someone once said that there are 1,000 uses. Here are a few suggestions.

Soup

Mint leaves are a fragrant and flavorful garnish for soups, especially split pea or lentil soup, also any cream soup.

Cheese

Add minced fresh mint leaves to soft cheese or to yogurt. Sprinkle it on sliced cheese in a sandwich.

Salads

Mint leaves, perhaps cut a little, can well be added to fruit or gelatin salads. They are fine as well in salad dressing or as a garnish.

Desserts

Mint is a delightful addition to apple pie. Use fresh leaves, finely minced, and add them to the filling and to the crust. They are equally good cooked in apple sauce or added to any apple dessert; also with peaches, pears, or other fruits. Good, too, sprinkled on custards and cornstarch desserts or on ice cream.

Drinks

As described above, mint is fine in chocolate; it is good, too, in coffee or coffee substitutes, also in tea or used alone to make an herb tea. Float a leaf or two on top of a glass of lemonade or punch.

See also Lemon Verbena; Apple Pie (Anise), Chocolate Cookies (Lemon Verbena), Comfrey Tea, Sugarless Cookies (Cardamom), A Summertime Drink (Comfrey); *and* Herb Butter, Candied Leaves, Candy, Herb Honey, Herb Jelly, Herb Sugar, Herb Syrup, Herb Tea.

Nasturtium *Tropaeolum majus*

Although many of our herbs originated around the Mediterranean region, the nasturtium did not. It was brought to Europe from the Indies or South America before or during the 16th century; in the 16th century it was mentioned in a book with the title *Joyous News out of the New Found World.* Nasturtiums were joyously welcomed for the beauty of their flowers; one author wrote of the nasturtium: "It is of so great beauty and sweetness . . . that my gardens of delight [that is the gardens not for medicinal purposes] cannot be unfurnished of it." Their gay colors and ease of growing has made them popular with home gardeners in many countries for many centuries.

Their culinary values were also recognized. A recipe for pickling nasturtium seeds appeared in *The Compleat Housewife* in 1736. It was soon learned that the flowers floated in tea or iced drinks added a festive touch; also that the flowers, leaves, stems, and seeds had a pleasant peppery flavor that added zest to salads and sandwiches. At least in the United States there was a lull for some time in the use of herbs. They were considered almost a necessity by the pioneers but then were replaced by spices. With the increasing interest in natural foods they have again become popular. Nasturtiums are among those gaining in popularity. One herb writer in 1953 listed nasturtiums among the twenty-four herbs she considered basic. Recipes for nasturtiums in food can now be found in a number of cookbooks.

Pickled seeds are served with lamb, mutton, and fish dishes. Seeds, either fresh or pickled, are added to pickles, potato salad, cottage cheese, and meat sauces. Flowers again appear as a garnish for salads, desserts, or floating in iced tea and fruit punch. Young leaves, chopped or whole, are a tantalizing ingredient in tossed salads, also in hearty meat, fish, or chicken salads.

While not related to watercress (*Nasturtium officinale*), nasturtiums have the same bright peppery taste and can be used wherever watercress is called for. Both, because of their pungency, have been called "Indian Cress," also "nose twister."

I am including no salad recipes, as you can add nasturtiums as an ingredient or a garnish to almost any of your favorite salads. Here are a few other recipes you may like to try. Seeds should be gathered soon after the flowers fall off. Buds and blossoms can be used until about to wither. Leaves should be young, also stems. I have watched a whole bouquet disappear from the dining room table as each child sampled the flowers—the beauty of the centerpiece could not compete with the happiness on the faces as they enjoyed the tingling delightful taste of the nasturtiums.

Pickled Nasturtium Seeds

During the last four centuries many recipes have appeared for pickling nasturtiums. The simplest one is to pick, wash, and dry the seeds (just put them on a clean towel for a short time). For each cup of seeds, dissolve 2 tablespoons salt in 1 cup of vinegar; add seeds, pour into sterile jar or bottle; seal; keep in a cool place. This is supposed to keep for a year and to be ready for use in a few weeks. This recipe calls for cold vinegar.

Another recipe, one that uses the same proportions of seed, salt, and vinegar says to pour boiling vinegar over the seeds. Still another suggests warm vinegar. I like best to bring the vinegar just to the boiling point, not actually boiling.

I like, too, recipes that call for soaking the seeds before pickling them. Some suggest adding other herbs—sliced shallots, chopped horseradish, and/or peppercorns; several call for one or more of these spices—mace, salt, pepper, whole cloves, crushed nutmeg. This is my recipe, but many variations should be just as good.

1 cup nasturtium seeds	2 tablespoons salt
Brine made with 2 cups cold water	4 whole cloves
and 3 tablespoons salt	1 cup vinegar

Wash seeds and soak in brine for 3 days, stirring well once a day. Then drain and put into sterile jars or bottles. Add salt and cloves to vinegar, bring to a boil, pour over seeds, and seal jars. Store in cool, dark place.

Serve over meat—especially good with lamb or mutton, also with fish or poultry. Try a little with beets or baked beans. If the pickled nasturtium seeds are stronger than you like, just add them to a brown sauce for meat or a white sauce for vegetables.

Pickled Nasturtium Seeds Meat Sauce

Season 1½ cups water or broth with salt and pepper. Melt 3 tablespoons butter, removed from the heat, stir in 2 tablespoons flour, and slowly stir in the water or broth. Return to heat and bring to a boil; add the seeds and simmer for a few minutes. Serve with meat.

Pickled Nasturtium Seeds Vegetable Sauce

Follow recipe above, using milk for the liquid.

Nasturtium Sandwiches

Probably the most attractive nasturtium sandwich is made by laying blossoms and a few leaves on a buttered slice of bread and serving it as an open sandwich. A more substantial sandwich is made by spreading one slice of bread with butter, another with cream cheese. Sprinkle the cream cheese generously with chopped flowers and leaves; top it with the buttered slice. Of course it is not necessary to chop the nasturtiums, but it is easier to eat. Mayonnaise can be used instead of butter or instead of cream cheese. Nasturtium flowers, with or without added leaves, are delicious sprinkled generously between the slices of bread in any meat, chicken, fish, cheese, or peanut butter sandwich. Use either white or dark bread; I like it best with whole wheat bread; it is good with rye. I saw one recipe that called for nasturtiums on top of a buttered slice of white bread and topped with a slice of whole wheat.

One does not have to use yeast bread in order to have a delicious nasturtium sandwich. What could be better than one made by crushing unripe seeds, mixing them with butter or margarine and spreading on steamed brown bread! Here is a recipe for the bread.

Steamed Brown Bread

1½ cups buttermilk	1½ cups whole wheat flour
½ cup corn meal	1 cup flour
2 tablespoons cooking oil	1 teaspoon salt
1 egg	1 teaspoon soda
½ cup molasses	1½ teaspoons baking powder

Put buttermilk and cornmeal into mixing bowl and let stand 10 minutes. Add oil, egg, molasses, and whole wheat flour; mix well. Sift in white flour, salt, soda, and baking powder, and again stir well. Have 2 or 3 inches of boiling water in a kettle large enough to hold the containers in which you will steam the bread. (I use empty tin cans that have the top completely removed.) Grease containers well, spoon in batter, filling no more than ⅔ full. Cover tightly with greased foil. Warning—do not have too much water in the kettle or the cans may tip over; but check occasionally to see whether more water is needed. Steam 2–3 hours, depending on size of containers. The longer it steams, the better the bread. Let bread stand 10 minutes before removing from container, so it will come out more readily. Warm in oven a few minutes before serving. This is the bread I like with nasturtium butter, but it is good with any spread or no spread.

Oregano

Oregano *Origanum vulgare*

Oregano is another fragrant and flavorful member of the mint family. Other names for it are origano, pot marjoram, Greek thyme, wintersweet. It has also been called "delight of the mountain." With its clean, sharp, pungent odor it is easy to understand why it was, in ancient times, a favorite strewing herb; also why, before the days of hops for brewing it was used in making ale and beer. The wild oregano we grew in our Ithaca garden was a weak-stemmed plant, 2 or 3 feet tall, with lovely purplish flowers. It had a delightful fragrance and a fine flavor. We found it growing wild; women who had used oregano in Mexico said the taste was the same— somewhat like marjoram only stronger and also somewhat like thyme.

The plants I have now came from a commercial grower. They are sturdy small bushes, also with purplish or pinkish flowers and with leaves that last all winter; giving an ever-ready source of spicy flavoring for any cheese, egg, meat, or poultry dish, also for many vegetables. They are good in soups, stews, sauces, and salads. Oregano butter, made by crushing the leaves and mixing them in softened butter, is good to spread on fish or meat, good, too, on French bread. Like most culinary herbs, oregano makes a good tea or is a good addition to regular or mint tea. Some like the tender young tips cooked as greens. They really are good, but I like them better combined with other greens such as chard or comfrey.

Vegetables for which oregano has been recommended include beans of all kinds, broccoli and all other members of the cabbage family, carrots, eggplant, lentils, potatoes, and tomatoes. Try it with pickled beets or baked squash. I have found it excellent in lentil soup. Oregano is considered by many to be a must in Italian, Spanish, and Mexican dishes. I've read that pizza, spaghetti, and lasagna are responsible for the unbelievably large increase in the use of oregano in this country. It is said that within a decade sales increased 5,000 per cent. Perhaps that is largely because of pizza, but probably it is partly due to the magic of oregano when used with tomatoes, bean soup, grilled steak, roast lamb, shrimp salad, and other sea foods.

Here are some of my recipes. I hope you will like them and that you will try oregano in other foods. If you are not already using it, start with just a little less than recipes call for. It is truly a strongly flavored herb. Next time you may want to use a little more.

Pig's Feet, Peruvian Style

Carol De Cabrera and I exchange recipes. She lived for a number of years in Lima, Peru, but grew up near Seattle. We both like experimenting with recipes. She likes some of mine; I like some of hers. We both like tender, well-cooked pig's feet. I sometimes just cut the boiled meat off the bones and serve it with sauerkraut and mashed potatoes. She makes a tasty sauce for it, using 1 tablespoon soy sauce, 1 can tomato paste, ¼ onion finely cut, oregano, and parsley. Her recipe does not say how much of the herbs, but 1 teaspoon dried oregano or 1 tablespoon of fresh is enough; use a generous amount of parsley. I also add 1 cup water with tomato sauce. Heat this mixture slowly. When it is bubbly and the onions are tender, add meat and serve over boiled rice.

Minestrone Soup from Peru

Since Carol lived in Peru, I suspect she used oregano much more often than we do. Here is another of her recipes. I am giving it just as she gave it to me. "Speaking of cooking and such, now that winter's here I have had to revise my menu-making to fit the season again. No more salad meals and sandwiches but heavy on soups, casseroles, and hot sandwiches with gravy. Two days a week we economize and have chili con carne and minestrone. The minestrone I make isn't authentic, because I mix a pound of ground meat with a whole lot of mixed vegetables, add leftover vegetables plus a Spanish sausage or two, some oregano, and let it simmer. Here you can get cut-up (in sticklike shreds) vegetables very cheaply in the market; they consist of squash, turnip, cabbage, carrots, peas, beans, lettuce, and what-have-you; some have garbanzos (chickpeas) added. I always add onion and some corn to it." With her minestrone Carol usually served just a salad and fruit for dessert.

Glazed Onions

1½ cups small white onions	2 tablespoons sugar
½ cup water	1 teaspoon dried oregano OR
1 teaspoon salt	1 tablespoon fresh oregano
3 tablespoons margarine	

Cook onions 15 minutes or until almost tender in boiling salted water; drain. Melt margarine in skillet; add sugar; stir and cook until mixture begins to brown. Add onions and oregano and continue cooking, stirring often, until onions are the shade of brown you like.

Variation: Thickly sliced onions can be substituted for the small white ones.

Stew for Two

½ pound stewing beef	1 carrot
1 tablespoon fat	2 onions
1 cup hot water (more as needed)	2 potatoes
	¼ cup raisins (optional)
1 teaspoon salt	½ teaspoon dried oregano
1 stalk celery	

Brown meat in fat over low heat, stirring often. Add water; bring to a boil and simmer 2 hours. Add other ingredients; bring again to a boil and simmer 1 hour. This stew can be made ahead of time, stored in the refrigerator, and heated when wanted.

Chicken Cacciatore

This recipe was given to me by Joanne Droppers, my youngest daughter. I hope that she serves it at least once every time I visit her.

2½-to-3-pound chicken	1 teaspoon salt
¼ cup salad oil	¼ teaspoon pepper
½ cup chopped onion	1 bay leaf
1 quart tomatoes, canned, fresh, or frozen	¼ teaspoon thyme
½ cup dry white wine	½ teaspoon oregano

Heat oil in skillet; brown chicken lightly on all sides. Add remaining ingredients and simmer 1 hour or until chicken is tender. Serve with boiled spaghetti and grated cheese.

Variations: Some cooks add a carrot and a stalk of celery, sliced thin, after the chicken is browned. Some use sherry instead of white wine. I would omit wine and use water instead, but perhaps Joanne is right when she says "If you do that, it would probably be good, but it won't be Chicken Cacciatore."

Ralph's Pizza

Ralph Tryon, my oldest grandchild, was thirteen the winter I visited my second daughter and her family in Fairbanks. Ralph was already a good cook; I liked his cherry pie and chocolate cake, but best of all his pizza. Here is his recipe. "Heat oven to 425 F. Stir with fork 2 cups Bisquick, ½ cup milk. Roll dough into a crust ¼-inch thick and place on a greased baking sheet. Spread onto dough in order listed: ½ cup grated cheese, 8 ounces tomato sauce blended with 6 ounces tomato paste, 1 cup salami, ½ cup cheese cut in pieces, 2 tablespoons salad oil, ½ medium onion chopped. Bake 20 to 25 minutes. Serves 6." Ralph added this postscript after listing the ingredients: "If you don't have any Bisquick, use biscuit dough. It does not matter what kind of cheese you use although I used Romano and Mozzarella. I didn't put in the oil, meat, or onion because we didn't have any and the crust was full." He had already learned that a good cook adapts recipes to what is on hand. With the cheese he did not really need the meat; the tomato sauce and paste gave sufficient flavor without the onion; the oil would have added calories not needed; and his dough was all right with whatever was in the Bisquick. He could have added 1 teaspoon dried oregano, mixed with the grated cheese. I hope he adapts as well to all life's problems!

My Pizza

I like Ralph's pizza, but I especially enjoy baking yeast breads and other baked foods so I use this recipe more often.

1 package active dry yeast	1 cup boiling water
1 teaspoon sugar	3½ cups flour
¼ cup warm water	2 6-ounce cans tomato paste
1 teaspoon salt	¼ pound Italian sausage
1 teaspoon dried oregano	1 cup grated cheese
¼ cup margarine	4-ounce can mushrooms, drained

Dissolve yeast and sugar in warm water. Add salt, oregano, and margarine to boiling water. In 10 minutes yeast will be lively and boiling water cooled; then mix them together; add 2 cups flour; beat well; add rest of flour. Knead until light and springy; spread about ¼-inch thick on greased baking pans (this recipe fits a 12-x-18-inch pan plus a 6-x-9-inch one). Spread tomato paste on dough; place mushrooms and sausage on top; sprinkle with cheese.

Let rise 40 minutes; bake at 400 F. until lightly browned, about 20 minutes.

Variations: Other sausages such as pepperoni may be used, also onion, bacon, sardines, or anchovies. Cheddar cheese is good, but Italian types are even better.

Cheese Cookies

I thought that oregano could not be used in desserts but it is good in these cookies. This is a variation of a recipe from the Tillimook, Oregon, County Creamery Association.

½ cup grated Tillimook (or cheddar) cheese

½ cup brown sugar

1 cup ready-to-eat wheat flake cereal OR corn flakes OR graham cracker crumbs

1 teaspoon dried oregano OR 1 tablespoon cinnamon

¼ cup peanut butter

½ cup chopped dates

Thoroughly combine all ingredients; shape into small balls; roll in granulated sugar; dry on rack. Blender can be used to chop dates.

Variations: Use raisins instead of dates. Don't roll in sugar.

See also Batter Bread (Parsley), Cup a Soup—Green Peas (Parsley), Deviled Eggs (Chervil), Easiest Fried Chicken (Rosemary), Gazpacho La Quinta (Parsley), Macaroni for Salad (Comfrey), Potato Salad (Sorrel), Pot Roast with Thyme, Scrambled Eggs (Basil), Split Pea Soup (Basil), Thyme in an Oven Roast; *and* Herb Jelly.

Parsley

Parsley *Petroselinum crispum*

Parsley is probably the best known and most widely used of any of the herbs. It is a member of the parsley or Umbelliferae family, as are a number of other well-known herbs. We have already considered caraway, chervil, coriander, cumin, dill, and fennel. Parsley might be substituted in recipes given for these herbs. Parsley has been used in many ways for thousands of years. It was being cultivated in England by 1548. It was one of the plants brought here by early pioneers; it was considered a necessary part of their gardens.

Greeks and Romans strengthened their chariot horses (or so they thought) with parsley, and crowned the victorious drivers with parsley wreaths. Three nights a year they powdered their heads with parsley seeds to keep their hair from falling out. They ate the leaves before banquets to prevent drunkenness, after banquets to remove the odor of garlic. They gave parsley wreaths to their beloved as a token of affection, planted soft green carpets of parsley on graves as a token of respect. Parsley was for them truly a versatile herb!

It is still a most versatile herb. Like our ancestors we can chew the leaves to remove the odor of garlic. Like them we decorate our food with the dainty leaves; we are wise when we eat the decoration along with the salad or roast—parsley has a good supply of vitamins and minerals as well as a pleasant taste. As a culinary herb it can be used alone or combined with other herbs; it has the happy ability of combining flavors.

Parsley is a biennial plant, blossoming the second year. It is, however, usually planted each year because the leaves are not so good after it blossoms. The seedlings are slow to come up—it is said that they go down seven times to the devil before sprouting. Parsley can be purchased the year around in many groceries. In all but really cold climates it can be used from the garden even in winter; if not, it can be dried or frozen. If only a few leaves are picked at a time it can be used continuously, since new leaves are formed. Use the stems as well as the leafy part; they have the same flavor but more of it. There are over 30 varieties of parsley but only a few are grown for kitchen use. The flat-leaved variety has the most flavor but the curly-leaved are best liked for garnish. There is a turnip-rooted form that is a tasteful vegetable when cooked and served like other root vegetables.

I am giving few recipes, for it can be added to almost any soup, salad, vegetable, sauce for meats or vegetables, and casserole. Cut fairly fine or not so fine and added to melted margarine or butter, it is a good addition to macaroni and other pastas, mashed potatoes and other vegetables, baked fish, or hot beef sandwiches; also good with these foods if added to a white sauce. I like to use it with other herbs when I bake yeast bread; it is equally good in biscuits or muffins.

Usually I caution "Use herbs sparingly"; with parsley I say "Be generous." Instead of a teaspoonful of dried or a tablespoon of fresh parsley for a tossed salad, use a quarter of a cup or more. For tomato soup, chilled vegetable juice, and creamed soups, sprinkle a teaspoonful of finely cut parsley on each serving. For a delicious sandwich, mix at least a teaspoonful with cream cheese—better make two sandwiches apiece! Or spread bread with parsley butter.

Parsley Butter

2 tablespoons minced parsley
4 tablespoons softened margarine or butter

1 tablespoon finely cut onion
   (optional)
½ teaspoon paprika (optional)

Combine all ingredients well. Spread on bread or crackers; especially good on ham and rye-bread sandwiches. Also good on fried fish or steak; likewise added to creamed or mashed vegetables. Parsley butter is good with almost any vegetable, meat, fish, poultry, eggs, or mushroom recipe. But then, so is parsley without the butter!

Variations: Onion or garlic powder can be used instead of the minced onion, or finely cut leeks, shallots, or garlic.

Gazpacho La Quinta

Gazpacho is a thick, cold soup of raw vegetables. I learned about it from Lois O'Connor, when she served it one hot summer day to members of our local herb society in Ithaca. Lois said that she first tasted it at a little inn in Mexico (La Quinta). The soup is supposed to have originated in Spain, but variations of it are found along the Mediterranean, in South America, and Mexico. This is the version

that Lois served; she has given permission to use it, from her book
Of Tarragon, Thyme, and Tauvirg.

1 clove garlic
½ teaspoon salt
½ teaspoon oregano OR 2 tea-
    spoons basil
1 teaspoon paprika
1 teaspoon sugar
2 large, ripe tomatoes, peeled
    and cut up
¼ cup sweet green pepper, finely
    chopped

2 tablespoons olive oil
3 tablespoons lemon juice
¼ cup minced parsley
1 tablespoon wine vinegar
1 cup cucumber, finely diced
¼ cup sweet onion, finely
    chopped or sliced paper thin
3 cups V-8 juice
2 tablespoons small croutons or
    dry bread crumbs

Crush garlic in a garlic press, or sieve it. Combine first 5 ingredients
with cut-up tomato and minced green pepper. Mix well, mashing
tomato and pepper. Add olive oil slowly, blending thoroughly. Add
remaining ingredients and mix well. If cucumber is garden fresh,
don't peel; if older, peel and remove any large seeds. Let soup chill
at least 4 hours—overnight is better. Drop an ice cube in each soup
bowl before serving the gazpacho.

Fortunately Lois had second servings and gave us permission to
copy her recipe.

Cup a Soup—Green Peas

Yesterday I wanted something to add to hamburger, toasted herb
bread, carrot and celery sticks for a lunch for three. I consulted the
refrigerator and came up with the following.

1 cup frozen peas
2 cups warm water
1 tablespoon diced onion
5 large parsley leaves, shredded,
    stems and all

1 pinch dried oregano
½ teaspoon salt

Put all ingredients into blender and run a minute or two, stopping
several times so it will not get too hot. When vegetables are just
large colorful dots, stop blender, pour contents into a kettle, bring
to a boil, and simmer 5 minutes. Very good! I am sure that canned
or fresh peas could have been used instead.

Variation: Just cook all ingredients without blending.

Batter Bread

1 tablespoon sugar	1 teaspoon savory
2 yeast cakes	½ cup dried milk
1½ cups warm water	½ cup rye flour
1 teaspoon salt	1 cup whole wheat flour
1 tablespoon parsley	3 tablespoons cooking oil
1 teaspoon basil	1½ cups white flour, approximately
1 teaspoon oregano	

Stir sugar and yeast into water in large mixing bowl and let stand 15 minutes. Add salt, herbs, dried milk, rye flour, whole wheat flour, and oil. Stir until well blended; beat vigorously for 2 minutes; then gradually add white flour until almost too stiff to stir. Let rise 1 hour in warm place; beat down and let rise ½ hour, or until doubled in size. Put into 1 large pan (9½ x 5 inches) or 2 or 3 smaller ones— well greased. Let rise until doubled in size; bake at 350 F. until bread shrinks from side of pan and has a hollow sound if tapped on the side, about 45 minutes, depending upon size of loaf. Cover with foil if top becomes brown too soon. Remove from pan and cool on a rack. Spread margarine on the top while still hot if you want a soft crust.

Variations: If you like crusty bread, bake some of this in well-greased muffin tins, filling them about half full. If you are fond of rye bread with caraway, omit herbs and add, instead, 2 tablespoons caraway seed.

Parsley Tea

2 cups cold water	1 or 2 tea bags (optional)
¼ cup fresh parsley leaves OR	
1 tablespoon dried parsley	

To water add parsley, bring to a boil, and strain. Reheat if a hotter drink is wanted. Some herb tea lovers pour boiling water over parsley and tea (if adding regular tea) and let stand 5–10 minutes before straining.

See also Burnet; Deviled Eggs (Chervil), Egg Sandwich Filling (Shallots), Fish with Sorrel, Herb Bread (Savory), Herbed Beets (Anise), Pig's Feet Peruvian (Oregano), Potato and Leek Soup, Potato Salad (Sorrel), Pot Roast with Thyme, Scrambled Eggs (Basil), Sorrel Soup, Split Pea Soup (Basil), Stewed Chicken (Coriander), Thyme in an Oven Roast, Tomato Soup (Borage).

Poppy Seed *Papaver somniferum*
or *P. rhoeas*

Some say commercial poppy seed comes from the opium poppy (*P. somniferum*), some that it is from a variety of that poppy, and others that it is from an entirely different plant, field poppy or corn poppy (*P. rhoeas*). All are agreed that no matter which plant it is, no opium comes from the seeds; opium comes from a different part of the plant. All are likewise agreed that poppy seeds are not only safe to use, but are a very real help in seasoning many foods. They have a crunchy texture and a nutty flavor. They are for sale either whole or crushed. Whole they are the tiniest, tasty culinary seeds I know; even so, crushing releases more of their flavor.

The use of poppy seeds in cooking is not new. Back in the first century Pliny wrote that they were sprinkled on bread, using the yolk of eggs to hold them on. He also commented that the ancients (I wonder how long ago his "ancients" lived) parched the seeds, mixed them with honey and served them with the second course of dinner. Early Greek athletes ate the seeds, mixed with honey and wine, before competing in games. The poet Homer referred to the poppy as a garden plant. Magical powers were claimed for the seeds. One could scatter them in his shoes and walk unseen past his creditors. I'm afraid that poppy seeds in my shoes would not protect me from the tax collector, but I am sure that the seeds have magic power in the kitchen. I can understand how in Holland (one of the important poppy-seed-producing countries) families proudly pass on from generation to generation the know-how of poppy raising, just as other Dutch families treasure bulb raising.

Poppy seeds add a nutlike flavor to bread, muffins, rolls, coffee cake, cake, and cookies; either mixed in the dough or sprinkled on top before baking. Stir them into milk and eggs for French toast. Toast one side of a slice of bread, spread the other with poppy seed butter (see Herb Butter), and toast for a few minutes in the broiler. Add honey, marmalade, peanut butter, or cream cheese to the poppy seed butter and spread on any bread or crackers. Add 3 tablespoons of seeds to a graham cracker pie crust. Stir crushed or whole seeds into noodles, rice, or macaroni. Add them to fruit salads or gelatin desserts. Sprinkle on top of sour cream on baked potatoes. Stir into any buttered or creamed vegetables. There are so many ways we can use these tiny, flavorful bits of goodness, that we don't need special recipes; we can just add them to our favorite ones.

Poppy Seed Bread Sticks

I have made bread sticks with my homemade herb bread for several years for a weekly coffee hour at our Convalescent Center. I wanted some a little fancier for a church breakfast so I made them with poppy seed: Spread slices of bread generously with margarine (butter will do) and sprinkle on the seeds; press them in firmly with the blade of a knife. Toast for ½ hour at 300 F., or for a shorter time at 350 F.

Variations: Sprinkle with sesame seeds or with grated cheese.

Chocolate Chip Cookies

½ cup margarine or other shortening	½ teaspoon soda
¾ cup brown sugar	¼ teaspoon salt
2 tablespoons poppy seed	¼ cup wheat germ (optional)
2 tablespoons buttermilk	¾ cup rolled oats, regular or quick-cooking
1 egg, unbeaten	½ cup chocolate chips
1¼ cups flour	½ cup chopped nuts
1 teaspoon baking powder	

Cream shortening and sugar; add poppy seed, buttermilk, and egg; beat well. Sift in flour, baking powder, soda, and salt together; mix well. Add wheat germ, rolled oats, chocolate chips, and nuts. Mix well. Drop, a teaspoonful at a time, on ungreased cookie sheet. Bake at 350 F. 10–12 minutes.

Variations: Corn flakes or other flaked cereals can be used instead of the rolled oats, or several cereals can be mixed. Nuts can be omitted but, if so, add more chocolate chips. Use part or all white sugar instead of brown sugar. Caraway or fennel seeds can be substituted for the poppy seeds; or the cookies can be flavored with ground herbs or spices instead of with seeds.

Oatcakes

2½ cups quick or old-fashioned oats, uncooked	¼ teaspoon salt
½ cup sifted all-purpose flour	½ cup melted butter or margarine
2 tablespoons sugar	½ cup milk
½ teaspoon baking powder	1 tablespoon poppy seed (optional)

1. Grind oats at high speed in the blender, grinding a third of a cup at a time. Not every flake need be ground; a few may remain whole.

2. Combine ground oats, flour, sugar, baking powder, and salt. Stir in melted butter or margarine. After oats have been completely absorbed, stir in milk and poppy seeds.

3. Turn dough out on a lightly floured board or pastry canvas sprinkled with additional unground raw oats. Knead dough gently 4–5 times. Sprinkle top of dough with additional raw oats. Roll out to a 9-inch circle. Cut in 8 wedges.

4. Using a wide spatula, put wedges ½ inch apart on ungreased cookie sheet, lightly sprinkled with additional raw oats. Bake at 375 F. about 30 minutes, or till lightly browned. Serve warm, with jam if desired. Yields 8 servings.

I added the poppy seed to this recipe that Gladys Burns gave me. She also used ¼ cup sugar, ¾ cup butter, and 2⅔ cups oats—a little more of each than I do. Sometimes I roll the dough into a rectangle and cut it in strips approximately 1½ by 3 inches. These oatcakes are good for party fare where one wants a change from too many cookies; also good at meals or snack time.

Variation 1: For a plain oatcake, decrease the butter to ¼ cup and sugar to 1 tablespoon. Proceed as directed.

Variation 2: For a dressy afternoon tea, roll dough in a 9-inch square; cut in small squares; bake 20 minutes at 375 F.; and spread with marmalade glaze (made by bringing to boil ½ cup sweet orange marmalade). Serve warm.

Czechoslovakian Poppy Seed Cake

This recipe and the seeds to make it were a gift from Edna Krizek after I had talked to a Home Bureau Group on cooking with herbs. I wonder if herbs make a person share, as Edna did, or is it the sharing-type of person who uses herbs? The poppy seed she gave me was very special, for she raises it from seed brought from the home country. This is the recipe as she gave it to me.

½ cup butter	1 egg
½ cup sugar	1 ounce yeast
1 teaspoon salt	Grated rind of 1 lemon
1 pint scalded milk	6 cups flour

Dissolve butter, sugar, and salt in hot milk; cool. Add rest of ingredients, the flour gradually; mix very thoroughly. Cover closely and let rise until double in bulk. Roll dough quite thin and cut into 3-inch squares. Put a teaspoon filling (*below*) on each square. Seal by pulling two opposite corners and folding to center or just beyond, then third corner and its opposite. Let rise until very light and bake about 10 minutes at 400 F., watching the last few minutes for color and doneness.

Filling for Poppy Seed Cake

1 cup black poppy seed, ground	½ cup sugar
Milk	¼ cup raisins

In double boiler heat seed with milk, sugar, and raisins. Use enough milk to make a moist paste. It thickens as it cooks. If not sweet enough, add more sugar.

Variation: Whole poppy seeds may be used, but are less tasty.

Graham Cracker Pie Crust

1 cup very fine graham cracker crumbs	3 tablespoons sugar
3 tablespoons soft margarine	1 tablespoon poppy seed

Combine ingredients and mix well. Pat firmly in bottom and sides of pie tin, reserving ¼ cup to sprinkle on top of pie. Add filling; sprinkle top with cracker crumbs; bake according to pie recipe. Especially good with packaged chocolate pie mix.

See also Apple Pie (Anise), Cottage Cheese Plus (Cardamom), Sugarless Cookies (Cardamom); *and* Herb Honey.

Rose *Rosa*

You may not think of roses as herbs, but when herbs are described as plants used for their fragrance or for medicine or for flavor, roses qualify on all three points. Since prehistoric days they have been treasured for their perfume. Herbals of the 16th century refer to their medicinal values as have pharmacopoeias since then. For centuries roses held an important place in commerce; the French or Provence rose (*Rosa gallica*) was once worth its weight in gold in the Indies. The Romans enjoyed rose flavors in their foods and drinks—rose candy, rose wine, et cetera. They must have had a vast supply of rose petals, for they had many uses for them. Sachets of rose petals kept their clothes fragrant; they slept on mattresses stuffed with roses and bathed in water scented with rose wine, washed their hands at meals with rose water, spread a carpet of roses on banquet hall floors, gave garlands of roses to the guests at the banquets; and doves sprayed with rose water were released to fly over the banquet tables. Until the 16th century members of the French parliament were presented garlands of roses regularly by selected members of the aristocracy. (I wonder whether the atmosphere, and the resulting actions, would be different if our legislators were given rose garlands to wear during their meetings.) Roses have always symbolized happiness and love; they have been the inspiration for much beauty in literature and art.

I doubt whether we realize that we can use roses much as the Romans did, at least in ways that can bring us the same kind of happiness. For fragrance we can plant an old-fashioned rose by our front door—they have much more fragrance than modern ones. We can keep a bouquet or a rose potpourri in the living room. We can cheer a sick friend or comfort a sorrowing one with a bouquet of rosebuds. We can create a feeling of well-being with a fragrant cup of rose hip tea. (Rose hips are the ripe fruit of the rose.) But do we use them as freely as we might in cooking? Like the Romans we could candy the petals. We could make rose syrup or rose honey for fruit salads and desserts. We could have rose sugar for our cereals and rose butter for dainty sandwiches. We could make jelly with rose petals and jam with rose hips. We could surprise ourselves and our guests with rose tea or rose punch.

How could we do all this? By using our imagination and slightly altering some of our favorite recipes. Here are a few suggestions and a few recipes to help us find more joy in cooking by using the ever popular rose.

But first a CAUTION. Be sure the roses you gather have not been recently sprayed with a chemical—I could wish they had never been sprayed. Wild roses, if you can get them, should be safe. So should the petals or hips that you buy from a health or specialty store.

Rose Petal Sandwiches

Sandwiches can be made with rose petal, or rose hip, jelly or jam. Spread one slice of bread with peanut butter and the other with jelly or jam.

For a dainty sandwich, spread one slice of steamed brown bread, or any other bread, with strained honey, another with margarine or butter. Put several layers of fresh rose petals on top of the honey before adding the other slice, or use rose petal honey butter.

Rose Petal Pudding

1 cup cherries, fresh or frozen	¼ cup sugar
1 cup boiling water	1 tablespoon cornstarch
2 teaspoons dried rose petals OR	¼ cup cold water
2 tablespoons fresh petals	

Mix together all but cornstarch and water, and cook until the cherries are tender. Combine cornstarch and cold water, and slowly add to cherry mixture. Cook 2 minutes, or until thickened, stirring constantly. Serve hot or cold. Use more rose petals if you wish.

Rose Petal Ice Cream

1 package unflavored gelatin	1 cup boiling water
1 cup cold water	2 packages dessert topping mix
½ cup rose petals	(or 4 cups dessert topping)
1 cup sugar	1 cup cold water (or milk)
1 tablespoon lemon juice	1 teaspoon vanilla
½ teaspoon salt	

Dissolve gelatin in ½ cup cold water. Blend rose petals, sugar, lemon juice, salt, and remaining ½ cup cold water in electric blender until all is liquid—just a few moments. Add boiling water to gelatin and stir well; add rose petal mixture and stir to combine. Put into refrigerator until it begins to set. Beat topping mix, water, and vanilla until stiff (one package at a time), or use prepared topping. Combine in large mixing bowl with half-set rose petal mixture, beating with eggbeater until well blended. Put into freezer until frozen an inch or so from edges. Take out and stir thoroughly; a smoother ice cream results if stirred a second time. Freeze until solid.

I used petals of Damask roses. They are very fragrant; otherwise I would have used more petals. WARNING: BE SURE THAT THE PETALS YOU USE HAVE NOT BEEN SPRAYED.

Rose Petal Honey Butter

½ cup butter or margarine
½ cup honey

1 cup firmly packed rose petals with bases removed

Blend all ingredients on medium speed several minutes until chopped and mixed. Great on toast, bread, waffles, and such. Great folded into yogurt (with or without butter). Great as a base for icing. This recipe was given to me by Helen Ross Russell, who created it for her book *Beginner's Guide to Foraging for Dinner.*

Rose Petal Syrup

Put rose petals in a dish and barely cover with boiling water. If possible, use petals of Damask or wild roses. Let stand 24 hours. Squeeze liquid from petals and strain. Add 2 cups sugar for each cup of liquid. Bring slowly to a boil, stirring constantly until sugar is melted. Pour into sterilized bottles; seal.

Rose Apple Jelly

Put a few rose petals in the bottom of the glasses before pouring the jelly. The petals will float to the top. (*See* Herb Jelly.)

Rose Pectin Jelly

Prepare as for rose syrup, but do not add sugar. Measure and use syrup for liquid, following directions on bottle or package of pectin.

Rose Hip Jam

Gather plump hips after a frost. Wash, cut in two, remove seeds. Add 2 cups water to 1 pound prepared hips. Cook until tender. Rub through a sieve. Add 1 cup sugar and 1 tablespoon lemon juice for each cup of pulp. Cook slowly, stirring often, to the desired consistency. (Some like their jam thick; others want it more spreadable.) Pour into scalded glasses, cover with paraffin; if your jelly glasses do not have a cover, put foil or plastic tightly over the top.

In *Stalking the Wild Asparagus,* Euell Gibbons has an excellent recipe for uncooked rose hip jam.

Rose Hip Syrup

This recipe is from *Harvest without Planting,* subtitled *Eating and Nibbling off the Land,* a most interesting book written and published by Erika E. Gaertner (Mrs. Donald A. Fraser). Erika used hips of wild roses in her syrup, but roses from the garden, if not sprayed with poisonous chemicals, can be used; I use petals of the Apothecary rose. (I've just now interrupted my typing for a cup of Apothecary rose tea with a little honey added.)

2 pounds fresh, fully ripe, deep   3½ pints boiling water
　　red hips   1 pound sugar

Crush rose hips. Boil 2 pints of the water and pour over rose hips. Bring back to boiling point, then set aside for 10 minutes. Strain through a jelly bag. When all juice has been drained out, set juice aside, return pulp to the pot, pour 1½ pints boiling water over it, bring to a boil, set aside, and strain as above. When finished, mix the two extracts. Reduce by boiling to 1½–2 pints, add sugar and stir until dissolved. Pour into sterilized bottles and seal; for immediate use the syrup lasts quite well in the refrigerator.

Mrs. Fraser added this note to her recipe. "While in Northern Lapland, I have eaten a rose hip soup with slivered blanched almonds as dessert. At the time I understood this to be made from dried rose hips. It was much thinner than the consistency of our syrup, but it might be suggested that a similar concoction could be made from a syrup that was less concentrated. While I do not personally favour such desserts, it might appeal to some, especially ice cold on a hot day, or when a vitamin C supplement is needed." *Harvest without Planting* is dedicated "to Donald who tasted it all."

Rose Tea

Add 1 teaspoon crushed rose hips to 1 cup almost boiling water; simmer, do not boil, for 10 minutes. Rose hips have an amazing supply of vitamin C and you don't want to boil that away. Instead of rose hips you can make tea by simmering ¼ cup fresh or 2 tablespoons dried rose petals in 1 cup water for 10 minutes. In either case you can serve the tea as is or add honey and/or lemon juice.

Rose Punch

Combine equal parts rose tea and fruit juice; sweeten to taste. Or add rose syrup to punch. Fresh rose petals floating on each glass add a festive touch.

See also Herb Honey, Herb Vinegar.

Rosemary

Rosemary *Rosmarinus officinalis*

Rosemary, one of the most fragrant of herbs, has long been loved. Brides have long carried rosemary in their wreaths and given sprigs of it to their bridegrooms; it is still used at wedding ceremonies in central Europe. Students in ancient Greece wore rosemary while preparing for examination, as an aid to memory. The clean, strong scent of rosemary was supposed to be both a deodorant and a fumigant; it was strewn in hospitals and jails to protect against vermin and evil spirits. It was put in clothes closets to protect against moths. Rosemary has long been considered a necessary part of a flower garden. It has an interesting shape: leaves like a pine needle with green above and grayish white beneath, tiny flowers, usually a soft blue, shaped somewhat like miniature orchids. Rosemary is an evergreen perennial but where winters are cold it must be brought indoors. It is a satisfactory house plant but does not bloom freely indoors unless it has plenty of light.

Rosemary has been, and still is, a popular cooking herb, especially because of its warming, spicy flavor. It tastes a little like sage or lavender with a touch of ginger or camphor. Its fragrance, which when it is cooking makes the kitchen such a fine place to be, reminds one of pine needles and heliotrope. Rosemary sprigs added to the barbecue fire are supposed to enhance the flavor of steak or hamburger. I know that branches in the fireplace add to the cheerfulness of the living room. When my husband was bedfast, rosemary leaves simmering all day brought a feeling of the out-of-doors into the house; they may not have been useful as a fumigant, but the fragrance was welcome.

Rosemary is a most useful culinary herb. It can be combined with almost any food, adding a unique and tantalizing taste to each. It can be added to jelly, jam, sweet pickles, lemonade, fruit punches, and apple cider. (*See* Herb Butter *and* Herb Tea.) Put a little (not too much) in soups, stews, and sauces, in stuffing for chicken and turkey, in macaroni and other pastas. It is good in desserts—try it in gingerbread, cherry pie, and fruit gelatins. There are recipes for eggs, cheese, fish, poultry, game, lamb, pork, and beef; it is used commercially in some sausages and in some pizzas. It adds interest to many vegetable dishes. I've found references to rosemary seasoning for asparagus, cauliflower, chard, cucumber, eggplant, green beans, lentils, parsnips, peas, potatoes, spinach, tomatoes, turnips, and zucchini squash. I'm sure it would be good with other vegetables. The other day for a dish-to-pass supper I brought a parsnip casserole seasoned with rosemary. It was well liked. (*See below.*)

Rosemary Rolls

I first used rosemary in baking rolls. These rolls will be ready for the table in less than 3 hours from the time you assemble the ingredients.

1 cup thick buttermilk	1 teaspoon baking powder
1 package active dry yeast	2½ cups flour
1 tablespoon light brown sugar	2 tablespoons soft margarine or
1 teaspoon salt	butter
¼ teaspoon soda	1 tablespoon dried rosemary
3 tablespoons vegetable oil	(better use less the first time)

Heat buttermilk slowly over low heat until lukewarm. (If not done slowly, milk will curdle.) Sprinkle yeast over buttermilk; add sugar, salt, soda, and oil; beat with rotary eggbeater until well mixed. Add baking powder to flour and sift into liquid mixture. Stir in with a spoon and then work with your hands. Knead on floured board, adding more flour if necessary, until dough is smooth and satiny. Flour board again and roll dough lightly until it is a long rectangle about ¼ inch thick. Spread with softened margarine or butter, and sprinkle with rosemary. Roll up as you would a cinnamon roll and cut into about 1-inch pieces. Place in greased baking dish but do not crowd slices. They fit into a 9-x-9-inch pan. Cut ½ inch thick if you like them crusty. Cover with towel and let rise in warm place about 1½ hours. Bake at 400 F. about 20 minutes or until brown. Makes a dozen rolls when cut in 1-inch slices.

These are good with most menus, but especially fine with a hearty salad in summer and with meat loaf and cole slaw in winter. I often double the recipe, as the rolls are good warmed up.

Rosemary Muffins

1 cup unbleached flour	½ teaspoon dried rosemary
1 cup whole wheat flour	¼ cup cooking oil
1 teaspoon baking powder	3 tablespoons molasses
½ teaspoon salt	1 cup milk

Sift together dry ingredients. Add oil, molasses, and milk, and stir until blended. Fill oiled muffin tins ⅔ full. Bake about 20 minutes at 375 F. The time will depend on size of muffin tins.

Scrambled Eggs with Cottage Cheese

2 eggs
½ cup cottage cheese
⅛ teaspoon rosemary

¼ teaspoon salt
1 tablespoon butter or margarine

Beat eggs until smooth, add cottage cheese, rosemary, and salt and blend. Melt butter or margarine in skillet, pour in egg mixture, and cook slowly. If heat is low enough, the eggs should cook in about 10 minutes. Either stir occasionally, or cover the skillet and cook without stirring.

Easiest Fried Chicken

Crush ¼ teaspoon rosemary leaves or break into small pieces; mix with 1 teaspoon of salt. Rub chicken pieces with margarine, sprinkle with seasoned salt. Place in well-greased shallow casserole, and bake at 325 F. uncovered 1 hour or until tender.

I was puzzled when I heard this called fried chicken, but it does combine cooking with fat and heat, so I suppose it may well be called frying. Whatever it is called, it is easy and very good. If a moister chicken is wanted, cover the casserole with foil; or wrap each piece of chicken in foil—but call this baked chicken.

Variations: Use dill, oregano, sage, or tarragon instead of rosemary.

Parsnips and Peanuts

2 cups cooked parsnips
1 cup white sauce
½ cup peanuts

⅓ cup grated cheese
1 cup cracker crumbs or bread
   crumbs

After boiling the parsnips 15 minutes, cool and peel them; slice into casserole. Stir in white sauce (*below*) and peanuts. Combine grated cheese and crumbled crackers and sprinkle on top. Bake 20 minutes at 350 F. Cover the casserole with foil until almost done.

Variations: Pecan meats, soy beans, or sunflower seeds can be used instead of peanuts.

White Sauce

½ teaspoon salt	2 tablespoons margarine or
1 teaspoon crushed rosemary	butter
OR 1 teaspoon finely cut	2 tablespoons flour
fresh rosemary	1 cup milk

Add salt and rosemary to milk. Melt margarine or butter; stir in flour; remove from the heat long enough to stir in milk; bring to a boil, stirring constantly. Pour over parsnips.

Variations: Other herbs can be used in the white sauce, and it can be used, with or without herbs, in other casseroles or for creamed vegetables.

Rosemary Delight

1 package lemon vegetable gela-	½ teaspoon rosemary leaves
tin	1 cup water
1 cup pineapple juice	1 cup marshmallows
1 cup grated pineapple	

Drain pineapple. Add water if necessary to make 1 cup juice. Dissolve gelatin in juice. Add rosemary leaves to water, bring to boil, and steep 5 minutes. Strain and pour hot water over gelatin. Stir until dissolved. Cool and put into refrigerator until it begins to set. Beat with eggbeater until light and foamy. Add pineapple and marshmallows. If marshmallows are small, use whole; quarter large ones with kitchen shears.

Rosemary Jelly

Add rosemary leaves, fresh or dried, to apple jelly instead of lavender (*see* Lavender Jelly). Or steep the leaves in water and substitute for liquid in recipes for pectin jellies (*see* directions on package or bottle of pectin). This jelly is fine to serve with ham or chicken, also with lamb or fish.

See also Lamb Stew (Leek), Pot Roast with Thyme, Sorrel Soup, Thyme in an Oven Roast, Zucchini Squash Casserole (Basil); *and* Herb Vinegar.

Sage *Salvia officinalis*

I suspect that more people know sage than almost any other herb. I was surprised recently to learn that sage is so well liked in America that we use a million and a half tons annually. How many tablespoons of seasoning is that! Thousands of tons are imported. Much of this is used by manufacturers of sausages and pizzas, but household cooks use a lot and not just for stuffing the Sunday roast chicken. For the Orientals, sage was a symbol of immortality. They liked it so well for tea that they used to trade 4 pounds of their tea leaves for 1 pound of dried sage leaves. In Europe it was thought to prolong life. I like the statement made in 1662 by Sir John Hill that sage "maketh the lamp of life, so long as nature lets it burn, burn brightly."

Sage is another of our fragrant herbs belonging to the mint or Làbiatae family. And as with others, drinking or eating sage was supposed to restore and strengthen the memory and to quicken the senses. Greek physicians called it the magic herb. Because of its pungent penetrating odor it was also used in fragrance bags and potpourris. In the linen closet it was supposed to keep moths away; it was planted beside the kitchen door to keep ants out of the house. Sage vinegar was used as a preventive of the plague.

Sage probably was grown in every garden in Europe, and is now in many American gardens. The common garden sage is not restricted to the herb garden; it is attractive among the flowers and vegetables. Pineapple sage is especially lovely, with long spikes of brilliant red flowers late in the season. It does have a pineapple flavor and odor; the leaves of this sage are delicious in jelly, jams, and tea. I've placed them in the cookie pan and put a sugar cookie on top of each leaf. The leaves stuck to the baked cookies and the flavor was delicious.

A very good sandwich can be made by spreading any of the sage leaves on buttered bread. European peasants supposedly ate such sandwiches all through the month of May, when the leaves are at their very best. We are more likely to cut up the leaves and mix them with butter or use the leaves in baking bread.

Because it seems to cut fat, or counteract it, sage is especially good with pork. It is good with any meat, fish, or poultry; also with eggs and cottage or cream cheese. Crumbled leaves can be used in a marinade; powdered sage can be rubbed on a roast; stuffings with sage are placed inside fish or poultry. A bit of sage in dressing for hearty salads seems to blend the flavors as well as adding flavor. It is good in soups, stews, and gravies. Sage leaves, fresh or dried, are appetizing in vegetables. Just remember that sage has a really strong flavor and use only a little. Of course when you find out what a very little does to your favorite dishes, you may want to add just a very little more.

Sage and Cottage Cheese Bread

2 cakes yeast	1 teaspoon sage
2 tablespoons molasses	¼ cup vegetable oil
1¾ cups warm water	½ cup cottage cheese
2 eggs	1½ cups uncooked rolled oats
1 teaspoon salt	1 cup powdered milk
1 teaspoon lovage (optional)	5½ cups flour
½ teaspoon thyme (optional)	

Stir yeast and molasses into ½ cup of the warm water and let rise for 15 minutes. Add eggs, salt, herbs, oil, cheese, and rolled oats to remaining water. Sift milk with 2 cups of flour and add to egg mixture. Add yeast, molasses, and water mixture. Beat 2 minutes or until smooth. Gradually add flour until dough is stiff enough to knead. Knead 10 minutes on floured board, adding flour as needed. Let rise in greased pan in warm place until doubled in bulk (possibly more than an hour). Punch down, turn over, again let rise until double in bulk. Turn onto oiled board, let stand 10 minutes, form into loaves, and put into greased pans. Let rise until doubled in size. Bake at 350 F. until done, about 45 minutes.

Raised Corn Bread with Sage

2 cakes yeast	1 tablespoon dried and
2½ cups warm water	powdered sage
1 tablespoon sugar	2 teaspoons salt
1 cup corn meal	¼ teaspoon soda
1 cup cold water	¼ cup powdered buttermilk
2 eggs	1½ cups nonfat powdered milk
¼ cup vegetable oil	7 cups flour (approximately)
¼ cup molasses	

Dissolve yeast in ½ cup of the warm water; add sugar and let stand in warm place for 15 minutes. Stir corn meal into 1 cup cold water and mix well. Gradually add remaining 2 cups warm water; bring to a boil, stirring frequently; cook 2 minutes, cover, and let cool. Then add to yeast, stirring until well blended. Add eggs, oil, molasses, and sage; stir well. Sift in the salt, soda, dry milk, buttermilk, and 2 cups of the flour. Beat 2 minutes or more, and then stir in flour until stiff enough to knead. Knead 10 minutes, first on a floured board, then with board oiled. Put dough in a well-greased bowl at least twice the size of dough. Turn over so greased side is on top. Cover and let rise in a warm place until doubled in size. Punch down, turn over, and again let it double. It will take 1 hour or more the first time; ½ hour may be enough for the second rising. Poke down, turn out on oiled board, cover and let rise 10 minutes. Grease 3 pans 9 x 5 x 3 (larger or smaller pans can be used if they total the same). Shape loaves and put into pans. Let rise until double in bulk; 30 to 45 minutes in warm place. Bake at 350 F. about 40 minutes; cover with foil if they brown too fast. Turn out on racks and let stand until cold. Loaves come out more easily if allowed to stand a few minutes first.

Toasted Bread Sticks

Slice bread, spread with margarine or butter, cut each slice into 5 finger-sized pieces, toast until crisp and brown in oven at 275 F., half an hour or longer. Corn bread sticks are especially well liked at the patients' coffee hour in our Convalescent Center; but any bread, especially herb bread, is good.

Poultry Stuffing

¼ cup margarine or butter	½ teaspoon salt
1 medium onion, chopped	1 teaspoon ground sage
1 stalk celery finely chopped (optional)	¼ teaspoon pepper (optional)
	¼ cup hot water or chicken broth
4 cups dry bread crumbs	

On low heat, melt margarine or butter and sauté onions and celery 5 minutes. Combine with remaining ingredients. This amount will stuff a 6-pound chicken; double for a 12-pound turkey.

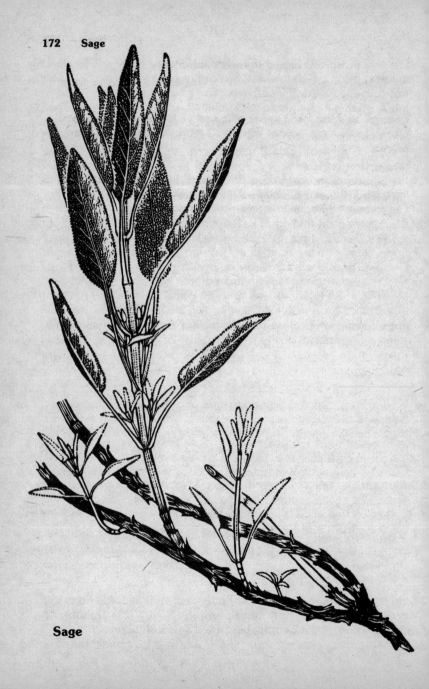

Sage

Tomato Omelet with Herbs

1 tablespoon salad oil	1 medium tomato, cut in pieces
½ small onion, chopped fine	

Heat oil in skillet. Add onion and sauté until golden; add tomato. Cook slowly until tender, about 10 minutes. Add seasonings as follows:

Seasonings

¼ teaspoon fresh minced sage	⅛ teaspoon summer savory
⅛ teaspoon fresh minced thyme	⅛ teaspoon salt
¼ teaspoon fresh minced marjoram	Dash pepper
	Pinch sugar

Cook slowly 5 more minutes. Add omelet mixture, beaten together, as follows:

Omelet

4 eggs	¼ teaspoon salt
¼ cup cream	⅛ teaspoon pepper

Cook slowly until firm; may be put in oven to set top. Serves 5. This recipe was given to me by Connie Lewis of Auraca (our Aurora-Ithaca Herb Society) before I left New York State for western Washington.

Chickpeas (Garbanzos)

Mix a large can (1 pound 14 ounces) of chickpeas with 1 cup tomato juice and 1 teaspoon sage. Bake uncovered at 350 F. for 1 hour or until almost all the juice has been absorbed by the peas. It can be cooked on top of the stove, but I like to bake it slowly.

Variations: Other vegetables can be substituted for chickpeas. And perhaps half as much sage would be enough. Be sure to use less sage if you have fewer chickpeas.

See also Easiest Fried Chicken (Rosemary), Herb Bread (Savory), Split Pea Soup (Basil); *and* Herb Jelly, Herb Tea, Herb Vinegar.

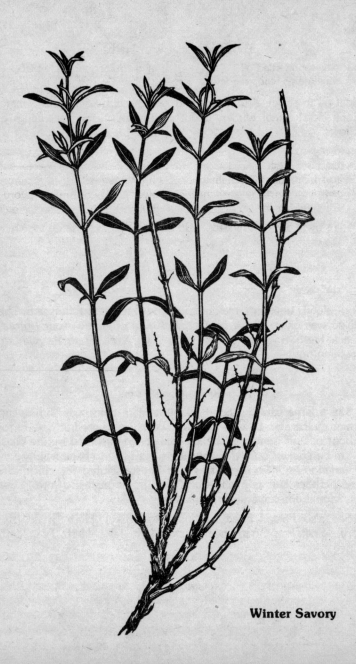

Winter Savory

Savory *Satureja hortensis* Summer Savory
        Satureja montana Winter Savory

Summer savory, one of the most fragrant and flavorful of the culinary herbs, and winter savory, equally fragrant and flavorful, are members of the mint family. Their use has been recorded in Europe for many centuries. They came to America with the earliest settlers and have been popular ever since. Winter savory is a perennial, well liked in rock gardens and flower beds. Summer savory is a rather weak-stemmed annual, but its profusion of small delicate pale lavender, white, or faintly pink fragrant flowers entitle it to a place in flower gardens. Savory is known as a bee plant because the bees are so attracted to it; the resulting honey has a hauntingly fine flavor. Furthermore a wet compress of savory leaves is said to give real relief for bee stings.

Sprigs of savory give distinction as well as fragrance to bouquets. The dried stems, if burned in the fireplace after their leaves have been removed, give out a spicy, balsamic scent. Savory was once used in medicine; it was thought to clear the eyes, improve the hearing, and aid digestion. It was supposed to awake the drowsy and brighten dull spirits. Today savory tea is still enjoyed for its aromatic peppery taste.

The English long ago used savory in puddings and pastries, in cakes and conserves. I like it in cookies; it is good in pumpkin pie, gingerbread, and apple butter. But it is used today more often with meat, fish, cheese, eggs, and many vegetables. It is especially good with all members of the bean family—peas and lentils as well as beans—in fact it is known in Germany as *Bohnenkraut,* in America as "bean plant." It can well be added to soups, chowders, stews, hearty salads, and meat sauces. In herb butter (*see* Herb Butter), it adds a piquant flavor to biscuits, dumplings, and scrambled eggs. It is supposed to be the very best herb with trout, excellent with all seafoods. When a few leaves are added to the water in which strong-flavored vegetables—onions, cabbage, turnips—are cooked, it really does improve the odor of the kitchen. When a few are cooked with canned beans (or other canned vegetables), it seems to take away the canned taste. As one herb-loving cook said, "It stings the taste buds just enough to bring out the flavors in the dishes it seasons." But just be sure you do not use too much at a time; its flavor is strong, somewhat like thyme or basil. One teaspoon of fresh leaves or ¼ teaspoon of the dried ones is enough for 4 servings. You may want less.

The following recipes call for summer savory. Winter savory has the same flavor but is stronger and less should be used.

Herb Bread

1 package active dry yeast	1 tablespoon vegetable oil
1 cup warm water	3 cups sifted flour
1 tablespoon sugar	1 tablespoon mixed dried herbs
1 teaspoon salt	

The herb mixture I prefer is 1½ teaspoons savory, ½ teaspoon marjoram, ¾ teaspoon parsley, and ¼ teaspoon thyme. Sprinkle yeast on warm water; stir well. Add sugar, salt, and oil, and stir again. Let stand 15 minutes. Add half the flour and all the herbs. Beat until smooth. Gradually stir in remaining flour. Place on well-floured board and knead until smooth and velvety (it takes about 10 minutes but it's really fun). Add a little more flour when necessary to keep dough from sticking to board. Place in greased bowl, oil top of dough; cover and keep warm until double in size (about 1 hour). Punch dough down in the center; fold in from edges; turn over in pan and let rise again until double (about 45 minutes). Shape into a ball; put on floured board; let rise 10 minutes. Shape into loaf; place in greased loaf pan 9 x 5 x 3 inches. Oil top of loaf. Cut 3 slashes lengthwise on loaf, about ¼ inch deep. Let rise until double in bulk. Bake at 375 F. until nicely browned, about 50 minutes. Remove from pan and place on rack to cool. Makes 1 loaf.

Variations: Sometimes instead of this herb mixture, I add 1 tablespoon dried and crumbled sage. Sometimes I add 1 egg and/or ½ cup powdered milk. I usually double or treble the recipe.

Cheese Fondue

3 egg whites	1 tablespoon vegetable oil
3 egg yolks	½ teaspoon salt
1 cup dry bread crumbs	½ teaspoon dried savory
1 cup milk, scalded	
¼ cup cottage cheese	

Beat egg whites until stiff. Beat egg yolks until lemon colored. Soak bread crumbs in milk. Combine all ingredients except egg whites, and mix thoroughly. Fold in egg whites. Pour into buttered casserole and bake at 350 F. 20 minutes or until a knife inserted in the center comes out clean. The baking time required depends on depth of casserole. This recipe I first used over 60 years ago.

Snap Beans with Savory

2 cups snap beans, fresh, canned or frozen	1 teaspoon fresh savory leaves
½ cup water	½ teaspoon salt
	1 tablespoon margarine

Cook beans in water with savory and salt until tender. Drain (save liquid for soup or a vegetable drink); add margarine. Garnish, if desired, with a few sprigs of savory (do not eat this garnish; it will be too strong) or with parsley. A long-time favorite.

Peanut Butter Refrigerator Cookies

2 cups self-rising flour	½ cup vegetable oil
¾ cup sliced dates	1 cup sugar
½ cup peanut butter, softened at room temperature	2 eggs
	1 teaspoon dried savory

Sift flour into mixing bowl. Blend in electric blender all ingredients except flour and dates. Pour into mixing bowl with flour. (Instead of self-rising flour, use 2 cups sifted flour and ¼ teaspoon each of baking powder, soda, and salt, sifted.) Add dates when all is well mixed, stirring in. Divide dough into two rolls, wrap in wax paper, and refrigerate until well chilled—overnight does this nicely. Slice as thin as you wish (I cut 4 cookies to an inch). Bake at 350 F. on ungreased cookie sheet 5–8 minutes. The length of time depends upon the thickness of the cookies. Really good.

See also Batter Bread (Parsley), Herbed Beets (Anise), Pot Roast with Thyme, Scrambled Eggs (Basil), Thyme in an Oven Roast, Tomato Omelet with Herbs (Sage); *and* Herb Honey, Herb Jelly, Herb Tea, Herb Vinegar.

Sesame *Sesamum indicum*

This herb, I've read, came to us not from Europe but with the
slaves from Africa. To them sesame was necessary as food and as
medicine; they also considered it a symbol of good luck. It has long
been a staple food in India and China. It was known in China as
long ago as 5,000 B.C.; its use goes back farther than that. An old
folk story tells that the gods of Assyria drank sesame tea to gain
enough strength to create the world. It does not say where they got
their sesame! That it does give strength was believed by ancient
Greek soldiers, who carried the seeds with them as emergency ra-
tions.

Sesame seeds are small, but they are very rich in protein and
have a good supply of minerals and vitamins. They provide one of
our best polyunsaturated fats. They have long been used in the
United States in medicines and cosmetics, recently in margarine
and cooking oils. They may have other commercial uses; in 1935
we imported 146,394,158 pounds of sesame seed as well as
11,088 pounds of sesame oil. Although we still import most of what
we use, it is being raised in some southern states; it grows well on
land that formerly was planted with cotton. Research is being carried on in Texas to find a sesame plant that will give a larger harvest
of marketable seeds. "Open sesame," the phrase used by the Arabian thieves in the Ali Baba tales, was appropriate—the ripe seeds
fall to the ground so quickly that it is hard to harvest them.

Sesame does not have seeds in northern gardens but is a decidedly lovely addition to a flower bed. It is a sturdy plant, 1 or 2 feet
tall, with long fuzzy tapering leaves and creamy white to deep lavender flowers shaped like small foxglove blossoms. It is not especially fragrant, but the seeds when toasted have a nutty fragrance.
They should be toasted to bring out the flavor unless stirred into
food before cooking. Sesame seed and oil are available at health
food stores and at many groceries. I buy the seeds by the pound,
for they add interest as well as nourishment to so many foods.

Sesame seeds can be used in any recipe calling for nuts, either a
substitute for the nuts or in addition to them. Combined with bread
crumbs, corn flakes, or whatever is used, they add value to the
topping for casseroles. They are a pleasing garnish for fruit salads
and gelatin or custard desserts. They add flavor and texture to rice,

noodles, pumpkin pie, or any apple dessert. They are a treat sprinkled on buttered bread that is to be toasted in the oven. They can be stirred into sour cream for baked potatoes. Sesame seeds are the bene or benne used in the popular Jewish candy Halvah. Toasted seeds are good with ready-to-eat cereals, salads, soups, casseroles, vegetables, desserts. Untoasted they go with vegetables about to be cooked; use only a little water and add butter or margarine. They add a nutty flavor to breads, cakes, cookies, cheese, chicken, fish, and meat. I can't think of any food to which they would not be a good addition. I agree with Dorothy Bovee Jones, who said in her book *The Herb Garden* that "sesame seed is indispensable and is almost universally liked." Here are some of the ways I like to use it. There are many more. I hope you think of some!

Cream of Wheat

1 tablespoon margarine or cooking oil	¼ cup Cream of Wheat
⅓ cup sesame seed	2 cups boiling water
	¼ teaspoon salt

Melt margarine in small skillet, add sesame seed, stirring occasionally, and cook over low heat 15 minutes. Slowly stir Cream of Wheat into salted boiling water and cook 15 minutes, stirring frequently. Remove from heat; stir sesame seed into Cream of Wheat, cover, and let stand a few minutes to blend flavors.

Whole Wheat Bread

2 packages active dry yeast	1½ teaspoons salt
1 tablespoon sugar	3 cups whole wheat flour
1 cup warm water	2 eggs
2 tablespoons margarine	¼ cup sesame seed
2 cups milk, scalded	4½ cups unbleached white flour

Dissolve yeast and sugar in water; let stand 15 minutes. Add margarine to milk and bring almost to a boil; let cool. Combine yeast and milk; add salt and whole wheat flour; beat 1 minute. Add eggs and sesame seed. Add white flour gradually, stirring as long as you can, mixing with hands when too stiff to stir. Place on floured board and knead until smooth, satiny, and springy (about 8 minutes). Work in more flour if sticky. Oil board for last half of kneading. Place in well-oiled pan, turn over so top is oiled. Cover and let rise in warm place until doubled, about 1 hour. Poke dough down, turn over, and let it again double in size. (This step can be omitted if you are in a hurry, but two risings give a finer texture.) Poke down again and let rise 10 minutes. Shape into loaves, either on an oiled board or directly from the bowl, and place in pans. The number of loaves depends upon size of pans; pans should be over half full. Let double in size. Bake bread at 350 F. 45 minutes, or until it is nicely brown and shrinks from sides of pan. Grease top of loaves lightly with butter or margarine; remove from pans; cool on racks. I think the baker is entitled to a well-buttered crust while it is still hot!

Variations: More sesame seed can be used if you wish, or caraway seed; or a tablespoon of ground coriander seed can be substituted for sesame seed.

Protein Sandwich Spread

2 tablespoons sesame seed, toasted
1 tablespoon margarine, softened

1 tablespoon strained honey
¼ cup peanut butter, chunk style or smooth

Combine all ingredients well and spread generously. Good on white, dark, or raisin bread. Especially good on graham crackers, Triscuit, or any other cracker.

Sesame Creamed Chicken

1 cup white sauce (*see* White Sauce with Parsnips and Peanuts *under* Rosemary)

½ cup diced cooked chicken
2 tablespoons sesame seed
1 tablespoon finely cut leek

Combine all ingredients and bring to a boil, stirring to prevent sticking. Serve on toast, rice, noodles, or other pasta.

Variations: Onions or any member of the onion family can be substituted for leeks. Sliced celery and/or carrots can be added, also a diced hard-boiled egg.

Fruit Salad

1 large orange
½ cup salad dressing
3 tablespoons toasted sesame seed

2 bananas, sliced
3 apples, diced

Section orange and cut sections in half, catching what juice escapes. Mix juice, salad dressing, and sesame seed. Combine fruits, add dressing, and stir lightly. Makes 4 to 6 servings.

Bene Wafers

¾ cup brown sugar	⅓ cup flour
2 tablespoons soft margarine	¼ teaspoon baking powder
1 egg	⅛ teaspoon salt
½ teaspoon vanilla	¼ cup toasted sesame seed

Blend sugar and margarine; add egg and vanilla; stir all thoroughly. Sift in flour, baking powder, and salt; mix well. Stir in sesame seed. Drop, one-half teaspoon at a time on a well-greased and floured cookie tray, widely spaced. Bake at 325 F. for 8–12 minutes. Carefully loosen cookies before removing; clean spatula frequently; if they harden too soon, return to oven for a minute. Removing the cookies is not easy, but is worth the trouble.

Herb Seed Cookies

Stir together 2 cups flour and a scant ⅓ cup sugar.
Stir together ⅓ cup oil and 3 tablespoons water.
Mix, sprinkling on more water if needed.
Roll ¼ inch thick; cut in small rounds.
Beat 1 small egg with fork.
Dip cookies in egg and then in sesame or fennel seed.
Bake on ungreased cookie sheet at 400 F. for 15 minutes.

This recipe was sent to me by Shirley Lindberg, a friend whom I know only through correspondence but who shares herb enthusiasm with me. She received it from a Chinese friend, Kao Ping-In. This cookie is ideal for after-school snacks for children and just as good for the coffee hour in our Panorama City Convalescent Center, where I like to furnish toasted herb bread sticks or cookies that are not overly rich.

Toasted Sesame Seeds

To toast sesame seeds, spread them not more than ¼ inch thick in a pan; bake in oven at 325 F. about 20 minutes, until lightly brown. Stir several times.

Or toast in a heavy skillet over a low flame until properly

browned, stirring frequently. They can be toasted at a higher heat, but must be carefully watched and stirred to prevent burning.

See also Cottage Cheese Plus (Cardamom), Poppy Seed Bread Sticks, Sugarless Cookies (Cardamom).

Shallot   *Allium cepa* Aggregatum Group

Shallots have long been popular in Europe, especially in France, where they are considered almost indispensable for gourmet cooking. They were once called eschalots, perhaps because they were brought by the Crusaders from Ascalon, an ancient city in Palestine. Like all onions they belong to the Amaryllidaceae family. By many they are considered the finest kind of the onion.

While we do not use shallots alone as a food—or seldom do—we find them an almost magical seasoning for salads, stews, soups, sauces, garnishes, and stuffings. Minced, with or without parsley, they are an attractive garnish for salads, adding a delicate onion flavor. As an herb butter they enhance baked or boiled vegetables. When not used in excess, they give a subtle taste to fish, poultry, and meat, also to cheese and egg dishes. They are reported to be the best of all onions for French onion soup. Shallot vinegar is milder and sweeter than garlic vinegar—excellent to use in homemade salad dressings. (*See* Herb Butter *and* Herb Vinegar.)

Shallots combine the best in the flavors of onions, garlic, and chives. Young garden onions, with small bulbs, are sometimes sold as shallots but they are not the best shallots; they lack the characteristic taste, which gives that gourmet flair to ordinary family cooking. Although, compared to some onions, shallots are sweeter and milder, they do have a definite flavor, and it is wise to use them moderately. Three or 4 shallots can be substituted for 1 medium-sized onion. A little adds so much to the enjoyment of food that it is a shame to ruin this enjoyment by using too much. They can be used in any recipe calling for chives, leeks, garlic, or onions. Wherever you use them, you may agree with the French that they are the most delectable of all onions.

Shallot Soup

1 cup shallots, finely sliced	1 quart boiling water
3 tablespoons margarine	4 slices toast
4 beef-flavored bouillon cubes	Grated mild cheese

Cook shallots slowly in margarine until limp and slightly yellow but not brown (they are said to be bitter if browned, but I have not tried it). Dissolve bouillon cubes in water, add shallots and cook, barely simmering, 30 minutes. The soup can be served after cooking a few minutes, but the flavor improves with longer cooking. Toast 1 slice of bread for each serving until thoroughly crisp. This can be done in the oven at 275 F., starting the toasting when you start making the soup. Rye bread is good, but any bread will do. Place a slice of toast in each dish, pour soup on top, and sprinkle with cheese (cheddar or Parmesan). This is my adaptation of a French Onion Soup I first tasted in a French restaurant in Montreal.

Variations: This soup can be made with any onion or onion relative such as leeks or scallions, but is exceptionally well flavored when made with shallots. Whatever onion you use, it may be wise to make enough for seconds and not plan much else for the meal.

Egg Sandwich Filling

2 eggs, hard boiled
2 tablespoons mayonnaise
1 tablespoon finely sliced shallots

A pinch salt
A sprinkling paprika

Slice and mash eggs, add other ingredients, and mix together. Refrigerate until wanted.

Variations: Grated carrot, finely diced celery, or sliced radish, or a combination of these, can be added; also parsley, chervil, or chives. Other salad dressings can be substituted for mayonnaise; other pepper for paprika; leeks or onion instead of shallots; or perhaps you would like a little garlic.

Cheese Souffle

¼ cup margarine or butter
¼ cup flour
1 cup milk
¼ cup thinly sliced shallots
4 egg whites

4 egg yolks
1 cup grated sharp cheese
1 teaspoon salt
⅛ teaspoon pepper

Make a cream sauce with 3 tablespoons margarine or butter, flour, and milk. Sauté shallots in the other tablespoon of margarine or butter until they are limp but not brown; they may become somewhat bitter if browned. Beat egg whites until stiff. Beat egg yolks, stir in cheese, salt, pepper, shallots, and cream sauce; lightly fold in egg whites. Pour into well-greased casserole. Bake at 350 F. until firm and lightly browned, about 45 minutes, but watch after 30 minutes.

Tuna Fish Salad

1 cup celery, sliced	2 cups tuna fish
¼ cup shallots, sliced	¾ cup mayonnaise
1 11-ounce can mandarin oranges	2 tablespoons mandarin orange juice

Slice celery and shallots; drain oranges and cut each section in half. Combine all ingredients and stir gently until well mixed.

Broccoli Casserole

4 tablespoons margarine	¼ cup thinly sliced shallots
2 teaspoons flour	3 eggs, well beaten
½ cup water	2 packages chopped broccoli
1 teaspoon salt	¼ cup dry bread crumbs
¼ cup grated cheese	

Make a white sauce by melting 2 tablespoons margarine, stirring in flour, adding water and stirring until smooth; add salt and cheese; stir until mixed. Melt remaining 2 tablespoons margarine, add shallots, heat, and stir until shallots are limp. Combine mixtures, stir in well-beaten eggs, add broccoli, pour into casserole; top with bread crumbs. Bake at 350 F. until firm, about 45 minutes.

Variations: The cheese can be sprinkled on top instead of being added to sauce; bread crumbs can be browned in 1 tablespoon of margarine and only 1 tablespoonful used for shallots; butter can be used instead of margarine of course.

Kale with Shallots

2 tablespoons shallots, minced	Cheese, grated (optional)
1 tablespoon margarine	Parsley, chopped (optional)
2 cups cooked kale	Paprika (optional)
Salt to taste	

Sauté shallots briefly in margarine but do not brown. Add kale; if it was not cut before cooking, cut before adding—I like to cut kale in fairly small pieces before cooking. Add salt if necessary; the amount will depend upon whether kale was salted when cooked. Heat but do not boil. Garnish with grated cheese, finely cut parsley, or a generous sprinkling of paprika. (Did you know that paprika is said to be a good source of vitamins?)

See also Leek; *and* Comfrey Soup, Fish with Sorrel, Horseradish Vinegar, Parsley Butter, Pickled Nasturtium Seeds, Potato Salad (Sorrel), Sorrel Soup.

French Sorrel

Sorrel

Sorrel	*Rumex scutatus* French Sorrel
	Rumex acetosa Garden Sorrel
	Rumex acetosella Sour Grass

French sorrel is the variety most often found in herb gardens. Both French and garden sorrel are listed in some vegetable seed catalogues. I know that garden sorrel and sour grass are found as weeds in many gardens. I hope the gardeners are aware of the food value of these weeds and occasionally use them when they are pulled up. Until I planted French sorrel in my herb garden, I kept a small patch of sour grass to chew while gardening; now I use the milder French sorrel. All three sorrels are well supplied with minerals and vitamins. All three contain oxalic acid which can add piquancy to soups and salads, fish, poultry, meat, and vegetable dishes. Because it is a little less acid and because its larger leaves are easier to use, French sorrel is usually chosen by cooks, but either of the other two can be substituted in recipes calling for sorrel—and in many recipes which do not mention sorrel but which could be improved by its sharp taste. Use it instead of vinegar or lemon.

Sorrel has been known since 3,000 B.C. For centuries it was popular in Europe; it still is, but only recently has been gaining favor in the United States. It was appreciated for its medicinal as well as culinary value for many ailments, especially scurvy. It also was a cosmetic: hands were washed in sorrel juice to remove stains; sorrel tea was drunk to improve the complexion. Housewives scoured pots and kettles with it, also bleached their linens with sorrel juice. Blossoms of sorrel are used in bouquets and dried for winter flower arrangements. Stalks with the seeds, picked before the seeds begin to drop, are especially attractive. French sorrel flowers and seeds are preferred because they are larger and showier.

It is the culinary use of sorrel, however, in which we are most interested. It was recipes for sorrel soup which I read in numerous cook books that first interested me in the plant and its seasoning qualities. Before that, I had thought of it as an interesting but not especially beautiful plant in the background of my herb garden. There were recipes that cooked the sorrel (briefly—it needs little cooking), cut up or whole, in chicken broth, beef bouillon, or water;

some that wilted it first in butter or margarine before cooking, that added onions or leeks while it cooked, that seasoned it with rosemary or nutmeg, that strained it or served it without straining, that garnished it with minced chervil or parsley. From these suggestions I concocted the following recipe for a soup which I like very much. You may choose a different combination of ingredients for your sorrel soup. Next time I may use chicken broth, may add a well-beaten egg or egg yolk after blending, may omit cheese. Remember that, if you do not have French sorrel, you can use sour grass or garden sorrel.

Sorrel Soup

2 cups coarsely shredded sorrel	3 cups boiling water
2 cups diced potatoes	⅔ cup dried milk
2 tablespoons diced onion (optional)	2 tablespoons grated or finely sliced cheese
1 teaspoon salt	1 tablespoon margarine

Cook sorrel, potatoes, onion, and salt in water 15 minutes. Add milk; blend in electric blender on high for 1 minute. Or put it through a strainer, or leave it whole. Add cheese and margarine; return to stove and bring to a boil. Serve with croutons or crackers.

Variations: Leeks or shallots could be used instead of onion. Add more water if you want a thinner soup. Sometimes I add a little nutmeg or rosemary, chervil or parsley.

Sorrel Sauce

1 cup sorrel leaves torn or cut into small pieces	2 tablespoons margarine or bacon fat
¼ teaspoon salt	3 tablespoons flour
½ cup boiling water	1 cup milk

Add sorrel and salt to boiling water; cook 3−5 minutes; drain and strain. Melt margarine over low heat; stir in flour; remove from heat; stir in milk; return to heat; add sorrel; cook over low heat, stirring constantly, until thick and bubbly.

Sorrel sauce adds an appetizing, piquant flavor served over bland fish, meat, or vegetables. Good also with fatty foods such as pork or duck.

Variation: Undiluted evaporated milk makes a richer sauce.

Fish with Sorrel

1½-pound fish fillet	½ cup grated cheese (optional)
1 cup sorrel sauce	2 tablespoons minced parsley
1 cup buttered dry bread crumbs	(optional)

Cut fish into bite-sized pieces; put into greased casserole. Pour sauce over fish; sprinkle with bread crumbs and then cheese. Bake until heated through and fairly well browned, about 25–30 minutes, at 375 F. Garnish with parsley before serving; or minced chervil, leeks, or shallots can be used. I use sole or turbot, but most kinds of fish would be good with sorrel sauce.

Sorrel Greens

Sorrel goes well with other greens. I like it with comfrey; it is good with spinach, chard, beet greens, or any other potherbs. If you like vinegar with your greens, you should like them combined with sorrel. One part sorrel to three or four parts other greens should be about right.

Sorrel with Vegetables

Remove stems and center ribs, chop or cut leaves and add to creamed vegetables, stirring them in; or use on top as a garnish. Sorrel is especially good with diced beets, baked beans, or any vegetable that might be served with lemon or vinegar. Add a leaf or two to the water in which carrots, peas, or other vegetables are boiled.

Potato Salad

3 hard boiled eggs, sliced	⅓ cup minced sorrel
2 cups diced cooked potatoes	⅔ cup salad dressing
½ teaspoon salt	

Combine all ingredients and mix well. Chill before serving. Taste to see if more salt, sorrel, or salad dressing is needed. You may want to add onion, leek, or shallots; I left them out as I like the flavor of sorrel. Other herbs can be combined with sorrel or used instead. Potato salad is good with almost any of the culinary herbs; tarragon, dill, basil, oregano, marjoram, chives, parsley, or chervil are suggested used alone or two or three combined.

See also Calendula; *and* Comfrey Greens, A Summertime Drink (Comfrey).

Tarragon

Tarragon   *Artemisia dracunculus*

This pungent herb, a member of the Compositae or sunflower family, came from the cold north, possibly Siberia, instead of the warm Mediterranean region, home of so many of our herbs. It spread slowly but steadily, by slips and root cuttings, since it does not bear seeds, and is now a favorite herb in many countries.

Tarragon's medicinal value was recognized as long ago as the 13th century, when El Baither, an Arabian botanist and physician, recommended that it be chewed before taking medicine because it dulled the taste and made the medicine more acceptable.

Three centuries later, the herbalist John Gerard wrote, "Tarragon is not to be eaten alone in sallades but joyned with other herbs, as lettuce, purslain, and such like, that it may also temper the coldness of them, like rocket doth. Neither do we know what other use this herb hath." Other uses, however, were found, and tarragon was grown, and still is, as an ornamental in flower gardens, as a dried flower for winter bouquets, and as an ingredient in potpourris and fragrance bags. Its chief use is in cooking. Many cooks consider it one of the most important culinary herbs; certainly there are few that can so easily add an alluring taste to ordinary, everyday cooking, can make a simple dish a gourmet's delight.

Tarragon has a strong, distinctive flavor. If asked what it tastes like I would have to answer "like tarragon." Writers have called it "somewhat spicy," "a little like anise or licorice," "appealing and satisfying," "rich and delicious." I agree with all this, but only if you use it a little less than moderately; too much and you would not want to use it again. I do not agree with the well-known 19th-century author, Dumas, that no vinegar is good without it. Tarragon vinegar is perhaps tops in flavor, but there are other good herb vinegars—burnet, mint, shallot, and thyme, to name a few. Nor do I agree with the enthusiast who claimed that every salad should be seasoned with tarragon.

Tarragon does add a pleasant flavor to a great many foods: to salads, soups, stews, sauces, vinegar, jelly, salad dressings, eggs, fish, chicken, steaks, tomato and other vegetable juices, raw or cooked vegetables including asparagus, artichokes, beans—snap, shell, Boston baked, limas, soy—beets, cabbage and all members of the cabbage family, mushrooms, spinach and all other greens, and tomatoes. Tarragon is excellent whether fresh, dried, or frozen. Just remember not to use too much.

Baked Chicken

4 chicken breasts	½ teaspoon dried tarragon
½ cup flour	1 tablespoon butter or margarine
½ teaspoon salt	2 tablespoons water

Put flour, salt, and tarragon in a large plastic or paper bag; shake to mix. Put chicken in bag and shake well until nicely covered with flour. Place in casserole, dot each piece with butter or margarine; add water. Cover (use foil if the casserole has no cover); bake at 375 F. until tender, 1 hour, more or less, depending upon chicken.

Variation: Use 1 teaspoon tarragon flakes sprinkled over chicken after adding butter, instead of mixed with salt and flour. Bake uncovered with no water.

Poached Fillet of Haddock

4 fillets, in serving-sized pieces	1 bay leaf
1 quart boiling water	1 teaspoon mixed culinary herbs
1 teaspoon salt	(optional) OR 1 teaspoon
1 tablespoon tarragon vinegar	your chosen herb (optional)

Add all ingredients to boiling water; bring to a boil, reduce heat, and simmer until the fish flakes easily when tested with a fork or toothpick, 4–8 minutes per pound of fish. Remove carefully, using a large slotted spoon. Serve hot, with or without sauce. Or chill and serve as a salad.

Variations: Use fillets of cod, perch, sole, or turbot.

Baked Carrots

2 cups carrots	1 tablespoon lemon juice
2 tablespoons margarine or butter	1 teaspoon salt
ter	¼ teaspoon dried tarragon

Peel carrots and slice, or if young ones, leave whole. Put in casserole; sprinkle with other ingredients. Bake covered until tender, 40–60 minutes at 375 F.

Variation: Peel carrots (or other vegetables), rub well with margarine or butter, season with salt and an herb, wrap in foil, and bake

1 hour or more until tender. This is good with ham cooked at the same time.

Cauliflower Casserole

1 10-ounce package frozen cauli- flower	½ cup milk
	2 tablespoons bacon fat
1 teaspoon salt	1 cup dry bread crumbs
¼ teaspoon dried tarragon	¼ cup grated cheese

Thaw cauliflower just enough so it can be broken apart; put into greased casserole. Stir salt and tarragon into milk; pour over cauliflower. Melt fat in a skillet; add crumbs; stir until well coated with fat. Top cauliflower with crumbs and sprinkle with cheese. Bake at 350 F. until nicely browned, about 30 minutes.

Variations: Other fats can be used instead of bacon fat, other herbs substituted for tarragon, other vegetables for cauliflower.

Lima Beans with Tarragon

1 10-ounce package frozen lima beans	½ teaspoon salt
	¾ cup water
⅓ teaspoon dried tarragon OR 1 teaspoon fresh tarragon, minced	1 tablespoon margarine or cook- ing oil

Drop beans and tarragon into boiling salted water and cook until tender, about 18 minutes. Add margarine or cooking oil and serve.

Variations: Omit tarragon and margarine from above; drain cooked beans and stir in a cream sauce to which tarragon and margarine have been added. Use fresh or canned lima beans instead of frozen. Try this recipe with lentils or chickpeas.

Cucumbers with Yogurt

1 large cucumber	½ cup yogurt
2 teaspoons salt	1 teaspoon dried tarragon
1 cup cold water	1 teaspoon lemon juice

Peel cucumber, slice thin, cover with salt and water. Let stand in the refrigerator 1 hour or more. Drain, dry, and stir into yogurt, which has been blended with the tarragon and lemon juice.

Orange Tarragon Jelly

1 cup water
1 tablespoon dried tarragon
3¼ cups sugar

1 6-ounce can frozen orange
   juice concentrate, thawed
½ bottle Certo

Bring water and tarragon to a boil and simmer 2 minutes. Let cool to room temperature. Strain out tarragon and add water to make 1 cup. Mix tarragon-water and sugar; bring to full rolling boil. Boil 1 minute, stirring constantly. Remove from heat, quickly stir in orange concentrate and then Certo. Blend, pour into glasses, cover with paraffin. Let stand at least 1 week before using.

See also Easiest Fried Chicken (Rosemary), Herbed Beets (Anise), Potato Salad (Sorrel), Pot Roast with Thyme, Scrambled Eggs (Basil), Thyme in an Oven Roast.

Thyme   *Thymus vulgaris*   Garden Thyme
         Thymus serpyllum   Wild Thyme

Thyme comes close to being our most popular herb. Wild thyme, also called lemon thyme, is well loved as a ground cover in rock gardens, flower beds, and even lawns. If you have ever stepped on it you will know why it is loved; you will agree with Kipling that the fragrance is like the dawn of Paradise. Besides being one of the most fragrant plants (some claim it is the most fragrant), it is loved for its beauty. Wild thyme in full bloom is like a living colorful tapestry. Garden thyme is about a foot tall, but not too tall to be a beautiful border for a flower or vegetable garden. Thyme is a most useful herb medicinally and commercially, and it is especially prized as a flavoring for a great variety of foods.

Centuries ago thyme was known from Siberia to Spain. It seems to grow in almost any climate. It was brought to our country by the colonists. Thyme in the bath water was supposed to increase a soldier's strength; I expect others used it, too, hopefully for strength and to calm the nerves. Just for enjoyment try adding a cup of strong thyme tea to your bath water. The best honey is said to come from regions where creeping thyme is the principal vegetation. There is no need to import bees to pollinate fruit trees, as some orchardists do, if there is plenty of thyme under the trees. What a joy to smell the fragrance while picking the fruit! We do not have so many woolens nowadays to protect from moths, but thyme alone, or mixed with wormwood and rosemary, gives a protecting fragrance to stored clothes and linens. Thyme in sachets and potpourris is a good herbal gift for invalids and shut-in friends. Thyme, a member of the mint family, is a hardy perennial, adding fragrance to the garden throughout the year. The flavor of thyme is just as delicious as its fragrance. As an extra bonus, one can enjoy smelling it while it is cooking. There is probably no herb that can be used with more kinds of food. Thyme blends well with other herbs, but use a little less of it than of others because it has a strong, penetrating taste. It is very satisfactory used alone and can be used as freely as salt, remembering that both salt and thyme should be used in moderation.

Thyme is an excellent seasoning for soups, stews, sauces, dips, fruit juices, salads, salad dressings, stuffing for fish and poultry,

eggs, cheese, fish, poultry, game, pork, lamb, veal, beef, vegetables, custards, fruit and gelatin desserts, jelly, herb butter, and herb

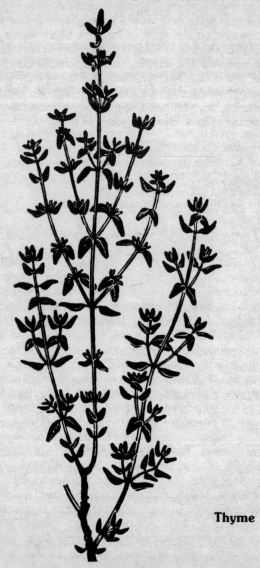

Thyme

vinegar. It has been especially recommended for these vegetables: beans, beets, carrots, mushrooms, onions, peas, potatoes, spinach, tomatoes, zucchini and other summer squashes. It is highly recommended for fruit pies—just soak 1 teaspoon of thyme in 1 tablespoon of lemon juice and sprinkle over the filling before putting on the top crust. Try thyme in clam chowder and oyster stew, cottage cheese and potato salad. Rub thyme butter on steak and fish fillets. Thyme tea, hot or iced, is refreshing after a busy day; stimulating before starting such a day; good to share with the children when they come home from school. Use thyme and imagination with any of your favorite recipes. Here are some of mine.

Thyme for Waffles and Pancakes

Sunday supper is waffle time at our house. Once friends arrived for waffles. The batter was ready. The waffle iron would not heat. I served the best pancakes I've ever made. Waffles are best with thyme; the same is true of pancakes. Served with tiny link sausages, maple syrup, and apple sauce they make such a good meal that it is hard to wait for Sunday evening. This is my waffle recipe, but you can add the thyme to your own favorite recipe.

3 egg whites	1 teaspoon thyme
3 egg yolks	2 cups flour
1½ cups milk	4 teaspoons baking powder
4 tablespoons vegetable oil	½ teaspoon salt

Beat egg whites until stiff, yolks until smooth-looking. To yolks add milk, vegetable oil, and thyme; beat with rotary eggbeater until well blended. Sift together flour, baking powder, and salt; add in thirds, stirring well after each addition. Now lightly fold in well-beaten egg whites. Bake in a preheated waffle iron. Makes about 6.

Pot Roast with Thyme

My favorite meat, I think, is pot roast. I often choose a boneless cut; if not, I make sure that the bone will fit into my iron Dutch oven or big iron skillet—my heavy iron lid fits either of these. Melt 1 tablespoon of fat, slowly brown meat on both sides, add 1 cup boiling water, and simmer several hours, until tender. At the end of 1 hour uncover, let it boil dry, and brown meat again on both sides. This step is not necessary, but seems to give more flavor. Add more boiling water and 1 teaspoon salt. An hour later add vegetables, placing them on top of meat: a potato apiece, an onion apiece, and several carrots cut into one-inch pieces. Later you may add corn, beans, tomatoes, and/or celery to the broth in which the meat is simmering. (If beans are not already cooked, they must be added at the beginning.) Sprinkle 1 teaspoon dried thyme on top of vegetables. This meal should be ready in another hour (about 3 in all), but cook longer if meat is not tender. Other herbs can be used with, or substituted for, thyme; any of these would be good—basil, bay leaf, chives, garlic, marjoram, oregano, parsley, or savory; or a very little fennel, rosemary, or tarragon.

Thyme in an Oven Roast

With a sharp knife make a number of small slits in the roast and stuff a pinch of thyme into each slit. Cook roast at 325 F. for 25–35 minutes per pound. I used to cover the pan and cook in a hotter oven. Now I leave the pan uncovered, place the roast on a rack, and remove it from the oven 15 minutes before time to slice it. Instead of inserting thyme in the roast, a couple of sprigs can be laid beside it in the roaster. Almost any culinary herb can be substituted for the thyme (*see the list given for* Pot Roast with Thyme).

Red Flannel Hash

1 large onion, sliced	2 meatless bouillon cubes
2 tablespoons margarine	½ cup liquid from beets
1 pint cooked and diced potatoes	½ teaspoon thyme
1 pint cooked and diced beets	Salt to taste
OR 1 can diced beets	

Wilt onion in margarine, but do not brown. Add potatoes, beets, and bouillon cubes that have been dissolved in liquid from beets. Stir until well mixed. Add thyme and salt to taste. Stir again and cook slowly until nicely browned. Remove from pan with spatula or pancake turner.

Variation: A can of ham or corned beef may be added with the potatoes and beets; the size of the can depends upon the amount of meat you would like. I prefer this recipe without meat, but I'm told that it cannot truly be hash if it has no meat, and Webster agrees with that.

Buttered Carrots

2 cups carrots	⅓ teaspoon ground thyme OR
¼ cup water	1 teaspoon fresh thyme
½ teaspoon salt	1 tablespoon margarine

Peel carrots and slice lengthwise or crosswise. Put into kettle with boiling water, salt, and thyme. Cover and boil gently 15–20 minutes, until carrots are tender but still somewhat crisp. Check once or twice to see that they do not burn; add more water if needed. Drain. Add margarine, stir, and serve.

Easy Baked Beans

1 large can baked beans	1 tablespoon pork fat
1 can dried onion soup mix	½ teaspoon dry mustard
½ cup unsulphured molasses	½ teaspoon dried thyme

Combine all ingredients and mix well. Bake in heavy covered casserole at 350 F. 30 minutes; remove cover and bake another 10 minutes. Add water if too dry at any time.

Rhubarb Coffecake

½ cup margarine	1 cup milk
½ cup sugar	1½ cups finely cut raw rhubarb
1 egg	1 teaspoon thyme
2 cups flour	½ cup sugar
2 teaspoons baking powder	1 tablespoon margarine
½ teaspoon salt	¼ teaspoon thyme

Cream ½ cup margarine and ½ cup sugar; add egg and stir until completely mixed. Combine flour, baking powder, and salt in sifter and add, alternately with the milk. Stir in rhubarb and 1 teaspoon thyme. Pour into greased 13-x-9-inch pan and sprinkle on topping made by mixing thoroughly remaining sugar, margarine, and thyme. Bake at 350 F. 30 minutes, or a little longer if not done.

Thyme Butter

Thyme butter is very good with waffles or pancakes that do not have an herb in the batter. Good, too, on fried, baked, or broiled fish; on fillets or steaks of fish or meat. (*See* Herb Butter.)

Cherry Thyme Jam

1 cup pitted sour cherries	3¼ cups sugar
½ teaspoon thyme leaves	½ bottle Certo
1 cup water	

Put cherries, thyme, and water in blender, run on low for a moment or two until cherries are slightly crushed; or cherries can be put through a grinder. Bring to boil and cook a couple of minutes; add sugar; again bring to boil, a full, rolling boil. Cook, stirring constantly, 1 minute; add Certo; stir; pour into jars; cover with paraffin.

This jam brought me a blue ribbon at the Thurston County, Washington, Fair in 1971. Just to encourage the use of herbs, I displayed a number of foods seasoned with herbs.

See also Burnet; Herb Bread (Savory), Leeks and Cheese, Macaroni for Salad (Comfrey), Sage and Cottage Cheese Bread, Scrambled Eggs (Basil), Split Pea Soup (Basil), A Summertime Drink (Comfrey), Tomato Omelet with Herbs (Sage), Zucchini Squash Casserole (Basil); *and* Herb Honey, Herb Vinegar.

Basic Recipes for Supplementary Foods

22 More Herbs to Cook With

Warnings about Using Herbs

Metric Conversion Factors

Basic Recipes for Supplementary Foods

Herb Butter

¼ pound butter or margarine (I use margarine)
1 tablespoon finely minced fresh herbs (OR 1 teaspoon powdered dried
    herbs OR 1 teaspoon herb seeds)
1 teaspoon vinegar (optional)

When making herb butter, start with just a little of the herb, taste as
you blend it, and add more until you have the flavor you like. It will
be easier to make if the butter or margarine is softened at room
temperature. Cream butter, add the herbs, and stir until well mixed.
Dried herbs will blend better if mixed with vinegar while the butter
or margarine is softening. Let both stand for an hour or two. Garlic,
leek, and shallot bulbs make excellent herb butter if finely chopped.
Leaves of any culinary or fragrant herbs are fine to use; you may
like to mix two or three kinds. Bread sticks from batter bread spread
with chive butter are popular with the patients at our Convalescent
Center Coffee Hour.

Herb butter is spread on fish, chicken, or meat; added to rice,
pasta, or any vegetable before serving; delicious, too, in sandwiches. Try basil butter in a tomato sandwich; mint, rose, or lemon
verbena in a tea party sandwich; oregano in a toasted cheese sandwich.

See also Calendula, Chives, Oregano; *and* Garlic Butter, Horseradish Butter, Rose Petal Honey Butter.

Candied Leaves, Flowers, and Seeds

I have not candied herb leaves or flowers, but I have received
them as gifts and know that they are delicious. Candied mint leaves,
rose petals, and borage and violet flowers are dainty additions
to a tea tray; fragrant-leaved geraniums should also candy well. To
candy them, stir 1 or 2 teaspoons of water into the white of an egg
(amount used depends upon size of egg). Hold the leaf or flower,
and with a soft brush paint it with the egg white, being careful to
cover all the surface on both sides; dust well with granulated sugar;

dry on a wire rack, turning when the first side is dry. Store in a candy box or other covered container. I have read that they may be dried in the oven at the lowest possible heat and with the door slightly open. For candied seeds, *see* Coriander Comfits. Other herb seeds can be used.

Candy

See Horehound Candy. Try making it with a strong tea of any of your favorite herbs. I think I would like basil or mint candy.

Garnishes

Parsley and chives have long been used to add beauty and flavor to salads, casseroles, chicken, meat, vegetables, and other cooked foods. Other herbs are also useful garnishes. I like chervil under or over a salad or anywhere else that I might use parsley. The flowers of woodruff, borage, and nasturtiums are quite lovely on desserts or in cool drinks. The leaves of burnet, coriander, and sweet cicely provide dainty garnishes for many dishes. The leaves can be used whole or minced; either way they are good to eat as well as to look at.

Greens

I raise several greens—chard, kale, and New Zealand spinach—in my vegetable garden for a succession of greens to cook for many months. But my favorites are in my herb garden. In the spring I like Good-King-Henry. Comfrey greens are good throughout the summer and fall; young leaves are the best, and young seedlings appear around the older plants. I have found references to the following herbs for greens: angelica, borage, burnet, calendula, chervil, chives, French sorrel, horseradish, lovage, oregano, sweet cicely, and woodruff. I think that young leaves of any of these would be good added as seasoning to spinach and other greens; I'm not so sure about them used alone. I think that one part of French sorrel to three or four parts of comfrey is better than comfrey alone.

Herb Honey

Herb honey can be bought at some groceries and health-food

stores or from herb dealers. I have seen fireweed honey and have read that horehound, lavender, marigold, peppermint, thyme, and other herb honeys are sometimes available.

Herb honey is easy to make. Keep the honey at room temperature for a while so that it will be easier to blend; or better yet, warm it a little over low heat. Stir herbs into the honey; warm over low heat for a couple of minutes; pour into sterilized jars and seal tightly. Leave in a warm room for a week before using, to let the flavors blend. Then warm over low heat until liquified enough so that the leaves can be strained out. Use the leaves of any fragrant herb: basil, borage, fennel, horehound, marjoram, mint, savory, and thyme have been suggested, also rose petals. Honey with ground herb seeds—anise, cardamom, coriander, fennel—would not need straining; whole poppy seeds also could be left in the honey. Suggested amount of herbs: 1 tablespoon of fresh leaves or rose petals, or 1 teaspoon of dried herbs or herb seeds, to 1 pint of honey.

Herb Jelly

Apple jelly with mint leaves cooked with the apples is my favorite way of making mint jelly. This is a fine method for making other herb jellies, too, although I sometimes use pectin instead. To make apple herb jelly use tart apples that are not entirely ripe. For 3 pounds apples (should make about 5 cups juice) use 1 cup chopped mint leaves. Wash apples, quarter them, remove stems and blossom ends, but do not peel. Put into large kettle and barely cover with water; simmer until soft. When almost done, add mint leaves which have been washed; stir well. Pour into dampened jelly bag and let drain until liquid no longer comes from the bag. Measure juice; add ¾ cup of sugar for each cup of juice. Bring to a boil, stirring until sugar is completely dissolved. Boil until a little on a saucer jells, or until it registers 220 F. on a candy thermometer. Pour into sterilized glasses; let cool; then cover with melted paraffin. If glasses have no cover, seal with foil or plastic.

Suggestion: If the apples remaining in the jelly bag are heated with a little water and then strained, you will have some good apple sauce; sweeten and perhaps add a little cinnamon or nutmeg.

For herb jelly without apples, use liquid pectin (or powdered pectin, if you prefer). Add ¼ cup lemon juice to 2¾ cups strong herb tea; bring to a boil; add 6½ cups sugar; stir thoroughly; again bring to a boil; add ½ bottle of pectin and bring to a full rolling boil (this must be cooked in a big kettle so that it will not boil over). Stir while it boils for 1 minute; then remove from the heat and pour into sterilized jars; cool, and cover with paraffin and with a lid, foil, or plastic.

I have not made herb jelly by placing leaves or flower petals in the bottom of the jar or glass before pouring in the jelly, but, if just a hint of flavor is wanted, that is an excellent way to do it; a nice leaf is sometimes placed on top, too. Almost any culinary or fragrant herb can be used. I have made jelly with at least eight different ones (used separately), but two or three can be combined. My favorites are horseradish jelly and orange tarragon jelly (*which see*). Others are angelica, basil, chervil, geranium (the fragrant-leaved ones), lavender, lemon verbena, marjoram, mint, oregano, rose petals, rose hips, rosemary, sage, savory, and thyme. (*See especially* Lavender Jelly *for a basic recipe.*)

Herb Salt

Whirl in a blender a minute or two 1 cup salt (without iodine) and 1½ cups minced fresh herbs; or blend several minutes in a mortar with a pestle. Spread on cookie sheet and dry in very cool oven with door slightly open. Blend again to be sure it is completely mixed. Store in covered jar.

Herb Sugar

Perhaps you have placed a stick of cinnamon in a can of sugar to have seasoned sugar for baking or to sprinkle on cereal or sweeten a cup of cocoa. You can do the same with any of the fragrant herbs. Put a pound of sugar—granulated or confectioner's, depending upon how it is to be used—in a jar that can be closed tight. Put a few herb leaves or flowers on the bottom of the container; sprinkle in the sugar, adding a few herbs at intervals. Use 8 or 10 rose geranium leaves—a corresponding amount of other herbs. Seal and let stand a couple weeks. Then sift out the herbs; take them out as you come to them; or crumble them and use with the sugar. This sugar is good in stewed fruit, baked apples, and other desserts, in cakes, cookies, cake icings, or sprinkled on top of cookies before baking them. If too strong, dilute it with unflavored sugar.

Herb Syrup

An herb syrup is easy to make. Dissolve 1 cup of sugar in 2 cups of cold water. Add a cup of fresh herbs, washed and crushed, or 2 to 4 tablespoons of dried herbs (depending upon the strength of the herbs). Bring slowly to a boil and simmer 10 minutes. Strain; pour into sterilized bottles; cork tightly. Any of the fragrant herbs can be used.

Herb syrup can be used to flavor tea, punch, desserts, and fruit salads. Sweet cicely syrup is good on apple salad; lavender syrup with custards; mint in cold drinks.

Herb Tea

I wish you could join me for a cup of herb tea; you could take your choice. I have twenty kinds of herbs in the kitchen that I use just for tea; about as many more that I use primarily for seasonings but that make excellent tea. I like them all but I probably use the mints most often—peppermint, spearmint, lemon or apple mint. I also like their close relatives—catnip, sage, and pennyroyal. Other members of the mint family that make excellent tea are basil, horehound, hyssop, lavender, lemon balm, marjoram, rosemary, savory, parsley, and thyme. Burnet, comfrey, costmary, lemon verbena, lovage, oregano, southernwood, and woodruff also are used for tea. Not all herb tea is made from leaves. Fine tea is made from borage, calendula, chamomile, and red clover blossoms; also rose petals and hips; Mormon or desert tea from the thin branches of joint fir (*Ephedra*); sassafras tea from the bark of roots; ginger tea from the roots of wild ginger; tea from the seeds of anise, caraway, dill, fennel, and fenugreek.

With some tea herbs boiling releases bitterness. Tea is often made by pouring boiling water over the herbs and letting them steep, closely covered, for 5 to 10 minutes. I usually put the herbs in cold water and bring it slowly to a boil; if it is not strong enough, let it steep a few minutes; then strain and serve. Cream or milk is seldom used with herb tea; honey or sugar is used by many; also lemon juice can be added.

How much herb to use depends upon personal tastes; I usually use 1 teaspoon of dried herbs or 1 tablespoon of fresh herbs for 2 cups of water. A strongly flavored herb such as fenugreek would need less; costmary and southernwood much less; parsley perhaps a little less; strawberry and raspberry leaves and most of the others would be just right—I've learned how delicious tea is when made from the leaves of wild strawberries. Woodruff, claimed by some to be the very best herb tea, is so mild that you would need to use more of it. Until you become a confirmed herb tea enthusiast, you may want to just add a few herbs to your regular tea before brewing. Or put some rose petals, a rose geranium leaf, or a few leaves of lemon verbena or rosemary in the bottom of your cup before pouring your tea.

I hope you do not wait until the doctor says "No more regular tea or coffee" before you learn the delights of fragrant herb teas.

Herb Vinegar

Herb vinegars are great in salad dressings—garlic for vegetable salads; burnet instead of cucumber; basil with tomatoes; mint or geranium in fruit salads. A tablespoon of herb vinegar (I use tarragon vinegar) in the water for poaching eggs improves the flavor and the shape of the egg; try it with poached fish. Pass an herb vinegar when you serve spinach or other greens. Mix a little in the filling for an egg salad sandwich.

I like to make basil, burnet, garlic, geranium, mint, and tarragon vinegar for gifts and bazaars as well as for my own use. I've read that at least 60 herbs can be used for vinegar; I've seen these, in addition to the ones named above, especially recommended: leaves of chervil, marjoram, rosemary, sage, summer savory, thyme; seeds of caraway, celery, coriander, and dill; flowers of clove pink, elder, lavender, and violets (I should think that rose petal vinegar would also be good); roots of horseradish and lovage; garlic cloves; shallot bulbs. Combinations of several herbs can be used.

For vinegar it is best to pick the leaves just before the plant blooms; the flavor is strongest then. I've made it sometimes later in the season, using more of the herb. Wash the leaves, pat dry, and fill a glass jar half full, pushing down and crushing them against the side of the jar (a wooden mixing spoon does this most efficiently). I heat white vinegar just to the boiling point, fill the jar to within two inches of the top, seal it, and place in a warm spot where it stands for two weeks; shake daily. I sample it then; if it is not strong enough, the leaves are removed and fresh ones placed in the jar; the vinegar is not reheated. Sample every few days and when strong enough, filter, pour into sterile jars and seal. Filter paper is recommended by many; I use two thicknesses of cheese cloth placed in a wire strainer. If mixture is too strong, it can be diluted with plain vinegar before bottling or when used.

Warning: Do not use a metal kettle for heating the vinegar; do not use a metal bottle cap. I coat my bottle caps with paraffin. I used foil once; because much of it dissolved, I threw away the vinegar.

While this is how I make herb vinegar, some make theirs with cider or red wine vinegar. Some chop the leaves before putting them in the jar—2 cups herbs for 1 quart vinegar. If you like to try a number of different herb vinegars you can use ¼ the recommended amount of herbs with 1 cup vinegar.

Flower, seed, and root vinegars would be made as above, using more of the herbs for flower vinegars, less for roots. If you use rose petals cut the white from the end of each petal—it is bitter. For herb seeds use 1½ to 2 tablespoons of seeds for 1 quart of vinegar.

22 More Herbs to Cook With

Other interesting herbs can be used in cooking, most of which I have grown in my garden. We have grown clary sage, but I have not used it because we had so much common garden sage. I have used, but have not grown, bay leaf and watercress. The following herbs I highly recommend.

Angelica, *Angelica archangelica,* is a member of the carrot, or parsley, family. It is a biennial, producing seeds the second year, but if not allowed to go to seed it may live for several years, dying down in the fall and springing up, bigger than ever, the next year. The large dome-shaped clusters of flowers, white or yellowish, make angelica a nice addition at the back of the flower garden. The leaves cooked alone, or better yet with comfrey or other leaves, are liked as greens. Candied stems are found in some confectionary stores. Well-crushed seeds are a good substitute for vanilla. In the long ago its fragrance was deemed a blessing; according to a legend in the *Rodale Herb Book,* an archangel revealed in a vision that angelica would cure the plague. In the early 1600's, Parkinson, an early British herbalist, wrote: "The whole plant, both leafe, roots and seed is of an excellent comfortable scent, savour and taste."

Bay, also called laurel, *Laurus nobilis,* is well liked with meat, fish, and poultry. One leaf, fresh or dried, improves almost any stew or broth. When I lived in New York State, I often used a leaf or two of **bayberry,** *Myrica pensylvanica*—it is also good.

Capers, the pickled small flower buds of *Capparis spinosa,* are a piquant seasoning in sauces for fish and meat, in herb butter for vegetables, and as a garnish for meat dishes and vegetable salads.

Catnip, *Nepeta cataria,* seems to make old cats as frisky as young kittens. It seems also to have a reviving effect on people—at least it is a favorite tea with some; others use a few leaves to season soups and stews.

A few dried flowers of **chamomile** (sometimes spelled camomile), *Chamaemelum nobile,* or of **German chamomile,** *Matricaria recutita,* are fine steeped for tea, or added to broth or to meat or fish soups and chowders, but if you use too many you will realize why Peter Rabbit's mother gave him chamomile tea when he got into Mr. McGregor's garden.

Clary, or clary sage, *Salvia sclarea,* is used like common sage. A teaspoon or less of the dried sage, or a leaf or two of fresh, is good in meat soups, also with cheese and with eggs. You might add a bit to the water in which you boil yellow vegetables—I've read that is good. I've also read that fritters made by dipping leaves of clary sage in batter and frying them are tasty. **Pineapple sage,** *Salvia elegans,* really does smell and taste like pineapple. Add it to fruit drinks and salads. Both of these sages make good tea, served either hot or iced.

I have used **costmary,** *Chrysanthemum balsamita,* only as a pungent tea, just right for a stormy afternoon; but I have read that it can be used in hamburger and other beef dishes; also that a leaf placed in the bottom of a cake pan would improve the flavor of pound cake. Costmary is also called Bible Leaf because it was used as a bookmark in the Bibles of our foremothers, and smelling it kept them awake during very long sermons.

Garlic chives, also called Oriental garlic, *Allium tuberosum,* is a milder flavored garlic. Its lovely white flowers can be used instead of parsley for a garnish, especially on salads. The leaves, chopped or cut, are good in tossed salad or on soups. Try them anywhere you would use chives.

Hyssop, *Hyssopus officinalis,* is a member of the mint family. Although grown mainly for its beauty in the flower garden, it is also useful in the kitchen. An invigorating tea is made from the fresh or dried leaves. They are also good for seasoning soups, stews, vegetables, and hearty salads; try them wherever you might use marjoram or thyme.

Lemon balm, *Melissa officinalis,* also known just as balm, another member of the mint family, known to be in use 2,000 years ago, can be used with soups and stews, with vegetables and meats, but is especially good with salads and desserts made with fruits, also with punch, soft drinks, and tea.

Two onions, not so well known as they should be but very good seasoners, are **top onion,** *Allium cepa* Proliferum Group (also called Egyptian onion), and **giant garlic** or Spanish garlic, *Allium scorodoprasum.* Both have bunches of small bulbils borne on stalks two or three feet tall. One small top bulbil can give an onion flavor to salads and soups. Giant garlic has a mild garlic flavor, good wherever you want garlic but not garlic of the usual strength. Young leaves of each can be minced and used like chives.

Oswego tea, *Monarda didyma,* also called bee balm, is a wild flower member of the mint family, cultivated in flower gardens and used for flavoring jellies, fruit salads, and fruit drinks. They make an especially pleasant tea.

English pennyroyal, *Mentha pulegium,* is a low mat-forming perennial with a delightful minty fragrance. Few people have known the joy of walking on a pennyroyal lawn; many can know the joy of drinking a cup of pennyroyal tea. **American pennyroyal,** *Hedeoma pulegioides,* an erect annual wild flower, has a similar minty flavor and will also make a fine cup of tea. The flavor as well as the fragrance is strong in both of these, so be sure to use only a small amount of the leaves.

Perhaps I should not list **purslane,** *Portulaca oleracea,* as an herb, but I want to include it here anyway, for it makes me happy when I can eradicate, or at least control, a thriving weed by eating it. Purslane, cooked with ham and seasoned with a little hot red pepper (or a milder seasoning), is one of the best summer greens.

It is not surprising that **saffron** is an expensive herb. It takes the stigmas of 4,000 flowers of *Crocus sativus* to make an ounce of saffron. The powder is often diluted with the stigmas of the annual **safflower,** *Carthamus tinctorius.* Either of these, or a mixture of the two, is used to give a rich yellow color to foods such as rice, bread, cake, and even some soups and sauces. Saffron adds flavor as well as color to meats and vegetables. A very little is needed; ⅛ teaspoon of ground saffron is recommended for a tea bread using 2 cups of flour.

Southernwood, *Artemisia abrotanum,* is reported as a flavoring for cakes and puddings. It has a lemony fragrance which suggests that it could be used in fruit salads and desserts, but I have used it only as a strongly flavored tea.

Sweet cicely, *Myrrhis odorata,* also called myrrh, smells and tastes like anise and licorice. Its delicate, fernlike foliage can be used like parsley and chervil, as a garnish. When I use the leaves under a salad, they are enthusiastically eaten. The same should happen to minced leaves used as a garnish on fish. The leaves also can be added to greens while cooking. The roots have been cooked as a vegetable for centuries and eaten raw for salad.

Watercress, *Nasturtium officinale,* grows in running water and is not found in herb gardens as a rule. It is a popular herb, available in many groceries in late spring and early summer. Use it as a garnish for soups and salads, fish and meat dishes; as a seasoning—pungent and peppery—in soups, salads, sandwiches, meats, and vegetables. Watercress can be a substitute for sorrel; try it in sorrel soup but don't use too much.

Woodruff or sweet woodruff, *Galium odoratum,* is a dainty ground cover with white starlike flowers. When stepped on, also when dried, it smells like newly mowed hay. Woodruff in wine is an ancient, but still popular, May Day custom in Germany, followed by many persons in this country. It also makes a tea with a delicate flavor and fine fragrance. The flowers are lovely on desserts or in cool drinks. And try a little with greens.

Warnings about Using Herbs

About rue, tansy, and wormwood, I wrote to the Liberty Hyde Bailey Hortorium at Cornell University, Ithaca, New York. The reply was that all three contain poisonous properties and their use can be dangerous.

Rue, *Ruta graveolens,* known as "Herb of Grace," is a beautiful plant—beautiful leaves, flowers, and seeds. But some people get a rash from touching the plant, and used in food it can be poisonous.

Tansy, *Tanacetum vulgare,* was formerly used as a seasoning in certain puddings and as a tea, but it is a poisonous herb, and use of the medical extract could be fatal.

Wormwood, *Artemisia absinthium,* also called absinthe, is used to flavor certain alcoholic drinks, but it is a poisonous herb.

Caution: Be sure you know your herb before you consider eating it. Especially when gathering plants from woods and fields, as with mushrooms be sure you are not confusing an edible plant with a poisonous one. Consult a good manual on identifying plants or an expert botanist before experimenting.

Metric Conversion Factors (Approximate)

Symbol	When You Know Number of*	Multiply By	To Find Number of	Symbol
	VOLUME			
tsp	teaspoons	5	milliliters	ml
tbsp	tablespoons	15	milliliters	ml
c	cups (8 ounces)	0.24	liters	L
pt	pints (16 ounces)	0.47	liters	L
	TEMPERATURE (exact)			
°F	degrees Fahrenheit	5/9 (after subtracting 32)	degrees Celsius	°C

*These are United States measures. The British Imperial measure system uses a 10-ounce cup and a 20-ounce pint. Adjust accordingly.

BOOKS ABOUT HERBS

INDEXES

Herb and Spice Cookbooks

Claiborne, Craig. *An Herb and Spice Cook Book.* Bantam Books, New York, 1965.

This low-priced copy of a book published by Harper and Row in 1963 is written "for everyone who wants to add a whole new vista to the joys of cooking and eating." Claiborne, a noted chef, starts his book with a chapter on basic recipes and then gives specific recipes for each of 54 herbs and spices. His recipes are clearly given for the beginning cook and delicious enough for the most skilled.

Gaylord, Isabella. *Cooking with an Accent.* Charles T. Branford Co., Newton Centre, Mass., 1963.

Enjoyment of this book begins with the table of contents. Happy anticipation is aroused by the chapter titles: "Herbs are the Accent," "Mints without Stint," "How Can a Man Die?" I've never been in Isabella Gaylord's kitchen but I feel as if I were visiting her as I read this book. As I read about the herbs and her recipes for them, my taste buds are tingling and I want to start cooking.

Howarth, Sheila. *Herbs with Everything.* Holt, Rinehart and Winston, New York, 1976.

Yvonne Skargon illustrates each of the 25 herbs in this book and adds 7 full-page colorful pictures of herbs with food. Sheila Howarth introduces each of the herbs and gives a fine collection of recipes.

Humphrey, Sylvia Windle. *A Matter of Taste.* Macmillan Co., New York, 1965.

The recipes in this book also make me want to leave the typewriter and hurry to the kitchen. But even if I weren't wanting to cook with herbs, I would enjoy reading it for the information about herbs. I appreciate her four-page bibliography, mostly books written in this century.

Mazza, Irma Goodrich. *Herbs for the Kitchen.* Arco Publishing Co., New York, 1973.

The purpose of this book is stated to be answering all your questions about cooking with herbs, even those you have never asked. The reader is introduced to 25 necessary herbs and told of 26 other useful ones and then given recipes for their use.

Miloradovich, Milo. *The Art of Cooking with Herbs and Spices.* Doubleday and Co., Garden City, N.Y., 1950.

This book is an excellent answer to the comment, "I'd use more herbs if I only knew more about them." There is a generous supply of herb recipes; also lists of herbs to use with basic foods—desserts, meats, vegetables, and so forth, as well as facts about herbs. Here is shared the knowledge acquired in a home where the use of herbs was a matter of course.

The following cookbooks were written by members of herb clubs. *Another Savory Seasoning,* 1969, has approximately 500 recipes discovered or adapted by members of the Western Reserve Herb Society, Cleveland. This is their third Savory Seasoning cookbook; a fourth is due in 1979. I wish there were more meals in a day so I could quickly try all their recipes.

I feel the same about *Accent with Herbs,* 1953, written by the Oregon Herb Society, Portland. They dedicated this book "to our Forebears who taught us the use of herbs," with the hope that it would inspire other cooks to learn the many fragrances and flavors that herbs give to otherwise common dishes. Though now out of print, the book is still available in some libraries and used bookstores.

Recipes for Foods with the Joy of Herbs, published in 1966 by the Southern California Unit of the Herb Society of America, Arcadia, Cal., has 100 recipes, also many "Have you used——with——" suggestions, for using "our garden herbs in new taste awakenings." More recently, they have published *Herbally Yours: Uses for Many Unusual Herbs,* 1977.

I also have two cookbooks by organizations that sell herbs. *The Herb Cottage Cook Book,* Washington (D.C.) Cathedral, 1964, was compiled by the National Cathedral Association and the All Hallows Guild. The 150 contributers include women from 50 embassies. What a delightful way to travel gastronomically around the world!

The Spice Islands Cook Book, 1970, by the Spice Islands Home Economics Staff is printed by Lane Books, Menlo Park, Cal. Besides a fine comprehensive selection of recipes it has an introductory chapter "The Romance of Spices," which includes herbs; "A Guide to Your Spice Shelf," which gives many interesting facts about the herbs; and three "Seasoning Charts," which tell what herbs and spices to use with different foods. I was especially pleased to see a chart for four herb vinegars.

Cookbooks with Herb Recipes

Many cookbooks use herbs in some of their recipes; some let you know which recipes by listing them in the index under "herbs." All have many recipes to which herbs can be added. The following, except the *Yankee Cook Book,* also have lists or charts that say which herbs can be used with different foods. The *Yankee Cook Book* does have a separate chapter on herbs.

Beard, James. *The James Beard Cookbook.* In collaboration with Isabel E. Callvert. Dell Publishing Co., New York, 1965; revised edition, Dutton, 1976.

Better Homes and Gardens New Cook Book. Meredith Publishing Co., revised edition 1976.

Day, Avanelle, and Lillie Stuckey. *The Spice Cookbook.* David White Co., New York, 1964.

Light, Luise. *In Praise of Vegetables.* Charles Scribner's Sons, New York, 1966.

Rombauer, Irma S., and Marion Rombauer Becker. *Joy of Cooking.* Bobbs-Merrill Co., Indianapolis, Ind. revised edition 1975.

Taber, Gladys. *Gladys Taber's Stillmeadow Cook Book.* J. P. Lippencott Co., Philadelphia and New York, 1965.

Vanderbilt, Amy. *Amy Vanderbilt's Complete Cookbook.* Doubleday & Co., Garden City, N.Y., 1961.

Wolcott, Imogene. *The Yankee Cook Book.* Ives Washburn, Inc., New York, 1963.

Woman's Day Encyclopedia of Cookery, Volume 6. Fawcett Publications, New York, 1966. This has a good article on herbs; others of the 12 volumes have recipes with herbs.

Herb Books with Recipes

Clarkson, Rosetta E. *Herbs, Their Culture and Use.* Macmillan Co., New York, 1966.

This is one of my most used books. I turn to the chapter "Tabular Paragraphs on 101 Useful Herbs" to learn how to grow or use any herb I want; and to the chapter "The Uses of Herbs in Cooking" if I want to cook with the herbs; it has good recipes and suggestions for use in my own recipes. The herb tables answer many questions about herbs in the garden.

Foster, Gertrude B. *Herbs for Every Garden.* E. P. Dutton & Co., New York, revised edition 1973.

For years Gertrude Foster, as editor of *The Herb Grower Magazine,* has given herb lovers inspiration and information. In her book she has brought together descriptions, culture, and uses of more than 150 herbs, including recipes for the culinary ones.

Fox, Helen Morgenthau, *Gardening with Herbs for Flavor and Fragrance.* Dover Publications, New York, 1970.

This is an unabridged and unaltered republication of her 1933 book. The first 75 pages strengthen our interest in herbs as we learn of the pleasures of an herb garden. In the next 190 pages we are introduced to 70 herbs that Mrs. Fox has grown in her garden—descriptions of each herb, history and legend, uses and culture. Then come the recipes with suggestions for herbal cooking. A bibliography has subtitles to make it easier to choose the books you want to read.

Hatfield, Audrey Wynne. *Pleasures of Herbs.* St. Martin's Press, New York, 1965.

An introduction giving a short history of herbal uses is followed by a discussion of some 43 culinary herbs, followed by recipes using these herbs. There is a section on toilet uses. The last section "Growing Herbs in any Garden" would be of help whether you were growing them on the window sill or in the flower bed.

Hersey, Jean. *Cooking with Herbs.* Charles Scribner's Sons, New York, 1972.

The subtitle of this book is *75 Recipes Using 15 Herbs You Can Grow Indoors.* The first chapter is "When, Where, and How"; I think it also tells "Why." A friendly introduction to each herb is followed by recipes. The illustrations are lovely.

Hogner, Dorothy Childs. *Herbs from the Garden to the Table.* Oxford University Press, New York, 1953.

How to grow and use 24 basic herbs should be no problem after reading this book, whether the reader is a gardener or a cook. There is much of interest about herbs besides growing them and cooking with them: ornamental herbs, medicinal herbs, growing herbs commercially, a list of herb gardens open to visitors, regional data, flavor chart showing which herb to use with 17 different classes of foods, bibliography. Nils Hogner shared his wife's love of herbs; the illustrations in this book are by him.

Hylton, William H., editor. *The Rodale Herb Book.* Rodale Press, Emmaus, Pa., 1974.

This organic gardening and farming book tells about using and growing herbs, "Nature's Miracle Plants." It has chapters by seven specialists. I especially liked the ones on the culinary herbs, on the healing herbs, and on companion planting—choosing and raising herbs that would repel pests and herbs that would help certain plants to grow better.

Jones, Dorothy Bovee. *The Herb Garden*. Dorrance & Co., Philadelphia, Pa., 1972.

"The Beginner's Herb Garden" discusses 10 essential herbs that should be in this garden. If you can't have them in a garden, you can grow them indoors. The next chapter adds more herbs for the experienced gardener. The recipes add delight to practical foods—I'm looking forward to making a strawberry omelet. A bibliography is included.

Lust, John B. *The Herb Book*. Bantam Books, New York, 1974.

This is a large comprehensive book on the growing and uses of herbs. A section "Herbs and Spices, the Art of Seasoning" gives good suggestions for the use of many herbs both as medicines and as food.

Schafer, Violet. *Herbcraft*. Yerba Buena Press, San Francisco, Cal., 1971.

On the cover it says "A Compendium of Myths, Romance and Commonsense." Mrs. Schafer claims a trinity of uses for herbs: "Meals, Medicine & Mystery." Myths and mystery are apparent throughout the book but they do not keep it from being chockful of commonsense; I think you will enjoy reading and using the recipes, and eating the resulting food.

Simmons, Adelma Grenier. *Herbs to Grow Indoors*. Hawthorn Books, New York, 1969.

If you want to grow herbs indoors, you are not limited to a few kinds. This book discusses 60 herbs, how to grow them and what to do with them, classifying them as herbs for flavor, for fragrance, and for fun. The first part of the book is entitled "Success with Herbs Indoors"; the second is "Recipes with Herbs." A few full-page illustrations show some of the places and methods for raising herbs indoors.

Sunset Book, Cooking with Spices and Herbs. By the Editors of Sunset Books and Sunset Magazine. Lane Books, Menlo Park, Cal., 1974.

This book combines an introduction to the culinary herbs with tempting recipes. It not only tells how to make herb tea; it has directions for adding herbs to coffee.

Sunset Book, How to Grow Herbs. By the Editors of Sunset Books and Sunset Magazine. Lane Books, Menlo Park, Cal. 1973.

This book begins with "The Lore and Lure of Herbs," tells how to grow and use them, has few recipes but many suggestions for their use in the kitchen. The final chapter "Favorite Herbs and How to Grow Them" includes illustrations and descriptions of each herb you are likely to use and why and how you would use it; you can then add it to your own recipes.

More Books with Herb Information

Bailey, L. H., and Ethel Zoe Bailey, comp. *Hortus Third.* Macmillan Co., New York, 1976. Revised and expanded by the staff of Bailey Hortorium, Cornell University.

Useful facts about herbs abound in this concise dictionary of gardening. If you look in it for information about an herb under its common name, you will be referred to the scientific name where you will find the information.

Clair, Colin. *Of Herbs and Spices.* Abelard-Schuman, London, New York, Toronto, 1961.

This is like two books bound in one. First there is an introduction to spices, followed by a discussion of 15, with a description of each and interesting comments about the plant. Over 70 herbs are included in the second part. Illustrations from a 16th-century herbal add beauty. Books mentioned in the bibliography cover centuries, from 530 to 1943.

Clarkson, Rosetta E. *The Golden Age of Herbs and Herbalists.* Dover Publications, New York, 1972.

This is a paperback republication of the book by Mrs. Clarkson first published in 1940 under the title *Green Enchantment: The Magic Spell of Gardens.* It has many references to herbs and their culinary uses: for example "Flowers in Food" and "A Prelude to Salads." It has a bibliography. It is a book about love of herbs and the beauty they give to life.

Clarkson, Rosetta E. *Herbs and Savory Seeds.* Dover Publications, New York, 1972.

This is an unabridged republication of the book originally published in 1939 under the title *Magic Gardens: A Modern Chronicle of Herbs and Savory Seeds.* Over 200 herbs are described in the final chapter. Preceding chapters give a gardener a working knowledge of different types of gardens and the herbs to use in them, their history and their use for medicine, fragrance, and flavor. Ten concise tables of herbs and an index "Books and Authors" add to the usefulness of the book.

Doole, Louise Evans. *Herb and Garden Ideas.* Sterling Publishing Co., New York, 1964.

This delightful book has many ideas for things to do with herbs for fun and fragrance and a few for food, especially party food.

Fox, Helen M. *The Years in my Herb Garden.* Macmillan Co., New York, 1973.

Helen Fox loved herbs and loved gardening. It is a pleasure to share her joy in her garden as one reads this book. Throughout are valuable comments on many herbs—what they look like, where and how to grow them. Full-page photographs, many taken in her garden, add much.

Gaertner, Erika E. *Harvest without Planting*. Published by the author, Mt. Royal, Quebec, 1967.

In this book Erika Gaertner tells of plants along roadsides, in field and woods, also of the wild animals, the fish, and the birds that she has served her family and friends and that they have liked. It was in this book that I found the recipe for rose hip syrup. There is also a fine recipe for sorrel soup and several for Jerusalem artichokes.

Gibbons, Euell. *Stalking the Wild Asparagus*. David McKay Co., New York, 1962.

—— *Stalking the Healthful Herbs,* David McKay Co., New York, 1966.

Both these books were written to encourage the use of edible plants growing in the wild, but many of the recipes are excellent for the same plants growing in gardens; examples are the rose omelet and the huckleberry pie. Adding gelatin, as suggested, to the graham cracker crust should certainly make it easier to serve.

Good Housekeeping Encyclopedia of Gardening (16 volumes, illustrated), Hearst Books, New York.

I turn to this for authoritative information on individual herbs—listed under their scientific names but also under their common names. Those most commonly used are also discussed under the title "Herbs." Under "Plant Finder" the last volume has a dozen lists of herbs for different locations and different uses.

Meyer, Joseph E., *The Herbalist*. Sterling, New York, revised edition 1968.

The name, description, and medical uses of many herbs are given. The illustrations in color of over 300 herbs are of interest as are the lists of dye herbs, tea herbs, flavoring herbs, and so forth.

Miloradovich, Milo. *The Home Garden Book of Herbs and Spices*. Doubleday & Co., Garden City, N.Y., 1952.

This book has no culinary recipes; these are given in his companion book *The Art of Cooking with Herbs and Spices*. It is a very real help, however, if you want to raise your own herbs in order to enjoy them directly from the garden or freshly dried for your cooking. It has an introduction to more than 50 plants with their characteristics, uses, cultivation, and harvesting; also chapters on growing, harvesting, and using culinary and fragrant herbs.

Muenscher, Walter Conrad. *Poisonous Plants of the United States.* Macmillan Co., New York, revised edition 1970.

I look up any herb new to me in this book to see if it is safe to use. I found warnings about three. (See rue, tansy, and wormwood in "Warnings about Using Herbs.")

Muenscher, Walter Conrad, and Myron Arthur Rice. *Garden Spice and Wild Pot-Herbs.* Cornell University Press, Ithaca, N.Y., 1955.

This is the first place I look for information about any herb. I like its concise and accurate treatment of the herb; also I like Elfriede Abbe's beautiful and accurate woodcuts; the models of many of them grew in our Ithaca herb garden.

Rohde, Eleanor Sinclair. *Culinary and Salad Herbs.* Dover Publications, New York, 1972.

This is an unabridged reissue of a book originally published in England in 1940 by Country Life, London. There is a short chapter on the planning and design of herb gardens. Forty-six herbs are discussed with comments on their use. Recipes are given, especially many for salads. Mrs. Rohde used about 20 different herbs to flavor her salads.

Rohde, Eleanor Sinclair. *A Garden of Herbs.* Dover Publications, New York, 1969.

This is another unabridged republication of a well-loved and authoritative book on herbs. Mrs. Rohde's bibliography lists books from 1440 to 1912. I am impressed that so many of my favorite herbs have been used for centuries. A recipe for "A Conserve of Marjoram" was in use 250 years ago. That is not her oldest recipe.

Simmons, Adelma Grenier. *Herb Gardening in Five Seasons.* Hawthorne Books, New York, 1971.

The preface "Herbs Are Forever—and For All" and the introduction "The Wide World of the Herbalist" indicate the scope of this book. The last chapter describes fifty herbs with their history, culture, and uses. The preceding chapters tell about the herbs most appropriate for each season, including recipes and suggestions for seasonal parties stressing herbs. The fifth season is Christmas.

Herbs

Scientific Names

Recipes using these herbs are indexed under the herbs' common names.

Allium ampeloprasum Porrum Group leek
Allium cepa Aggregatum Group shallot
Allium cepa Proliferum Group top onion
Allium sativum garlic
Allium schoenoprasum chive
Allium scorodoprasum giant garlic
Allium tuberosum garlic chive
Aloysia triphylla lemon verbena
Anethum graveolens dill
Angelica archangelica angelica
Anthriscus cerefolium chervil
Armoracia rusticana horseradish
Artemisia abrotanum southernwood
Artemisia absinthium wormwood
Artemisia dracunculus tarragon
Atriplex hortensis orach
Borago officinalis borage
Calendula officinalis calendula
Capparis spinosa caper
Carthamus tinctorius safflower
Carum carvi caraway
Chaerophyllum bulbosum turnip-rooted chervil
Chamaemelum nobile chamomile
Chenopodium album lamb's-quarters
Chenopodium ambrosioides epazote
Chenopodium bonus-henricus Good-King-Henry
Chrysanthemum balsamita costmary
Coriandrum sativum coriander
Crocus sativus saffron
Cuminum cyminum cumin
Elettaria cardamomum cardamom
Ephedra species joint fir
Foeniculum vulgare fennel
Galium odoratum woodruff
Hedeoma pulegioides American pennyroyal

Helianthus tuberosus Jerusalem artichoke
Hyssopus officinalis hyssop
Laurus nobilis bay
Lavandula angustifolia subsp. *angustifolia* lavender
Levisticum officinale lovage
Marrubium vulgare horehound
Matricaria recutita German chamomile
Melissa officinalis lemon balm
Mentha species mint
Mentha pulegium English pennyroyal
Mentha spicata spearmint
Mentha suaveolens apple mint
Mentha ×*piperita* peppermint
Mentha ×*piperita* var. *citrata* lemon mint
Monarda didyma Oswego tea
Myrica pensylvanica bayberry
Myrrhis odorata sweet cicely
Nasturtium officinale watercress
Nepeta cataria catnip
Ocimum basilicum basil
Origanum majorana marjoram
Origanum vulgare oregano
Papaver rhoeas field poppy
Papaver somniferum opium poppy
Pelargonium species fragrant-leaved geranium
Petroselinum crispum parsley
Pimpinella anisum anise
Portulaca oleracea purslane
Poterium sanguisorba burnet
Rosa species rose
Rosa gallica French rose
Rosmarinus officinalis rosemary
Rumex acetosa garden sorrel
Rumex acetosella sour grass
Rumex scutatus French sorrel
Ruta graveolens rue

Foods

WAYS TO USE TEN BASIC HERBS

Apple Mint
Oatmeal
Fish
Carrots
Snap beans
Fruit salads
Apple pie (also crust)

Basil
Waffles
Whole wheat bread
Corn chowder
Scrambled eggs
Chicken
Dumplings
Squash
Tomatoes

Chives
Clam chowder
Tuna fish salad
Deviled eggs
Meat balls
Rice (after cooking)
Buttered new potatoes
Tossed salads

Marjoram
Biscuits
Hamburger rolls
Dumplings
Scrambled eggs
Fried chicken
Hash
Scalloped potatoes
Tomatoes

Oregano
Beef soup
Scrambled eggs
Meat balls

Parsley
Vegetable soup
Scrambled eggs
Chicken
Hamburger
Potato salad
Tossed salads

Rosemary
Dumplings
Bread
Eggs
Chicken
Lamb stew
Roast beef
Snap beans
Rice

Sage
Cereal
Whole wheat bread
Chicken
Lamb stew
Meat loaf
Egg salad

Summer Savory
Eggs
Hamburger
Creamed potatoes
Snap beans

Thyme
Waffles
Pea soup
Scrambled eggs
Hamburger
Beets
Carrots
Snap beans

OTHER HERBS TO USE
Ground cardamom seed—breads and cookies
Caraway seed—beets, cabbage, bread, cookies
Celery seed—soups, breads
Ground coriander seed—potato salad, waffles, bread, cookies, pumpkin
    pie, cherry pudding
Cumin—clam chowder, chicken
Dill—fish, salads, peas, tomatoes
Garlic—vinegar, butter, meats
Lovage—liver, tossed salads
Sesame seed—orange bread, cookies
Tarragon—steak, tossed salads

TEA HERBS
Anise   Lemon verbena
Apple mint   Peppermint
Cardamom   Spearmint
Costmary   Sage
Fennel   Woodruff
Lemon balm

HERB MIXTURES
Celery seed and sage—bread
Oregano, chives, thyme—bread
Parsley, sage, oregano, marjoram, basil—bread
Sage, oregano, thyme—bread
Thyme, marjoram, chives, parsley—bread
Garlic cloves and tarragon sprigs—salad dressing
Thyme and rosemary—white sauce
Bay leaf, parsley, marjoram—chicken soup
Thyme and rosemary—chicken soup
Thyme, basil, oregano—barley beef soup
Chives, oregano, basil—boiled tongue
Myrtle leaf, parsley, marjoram—boiled tongue
Thyme, marjoram, parsley—deviled eggs
Thyme, savory, rosemary—tuna casserole
Rosemary and powdered coriander seed—chicken casserole
Myrtle leaf, rosemary, parsley, chives—stewed chicken
Parsley, savory, oregano, thyme, basil—meat and vegetable casserole
Basil and sage—hash
Basil, rosemary, savory—meat balls
Chives, savory, rosemary, oregano, basil—meat loaf
Thyme, parsley, rosemary—meat loaf
Bay leaves, chives, rosemary—stewed flank roast
Rosemary, chives, basil—pot roast
Thyme, basil, sage—scalloped potatoes
Rosemary, thyme, chives, parsley—rice

Notes

Notes

Notes

Notes

_____

_____

_____

_____

_____

_____

_____

_____

_____

_____

_____

_____

_____

_____

_____

_____

_____

_____

Notes

Notes

Notes

Notes

Notes

Notes

_____

_____

_____

_____

_____

_____

_____

_____

_____

_____

_____

_____

_____

_____

_____

_____

Notes